Praise for

SHIFT THIS!   W9-ARQ-259

"Joy Kirr speaks to you directly from the heart in *Shift This!* This is one teacher sharing her journey in an easy-to-follow format and striking narrative. If you've ever felt overwhelmed or frustrated at all of the changes in education, *Shift This!* is the book for you. Joy shares simple shifts that any teacher can use to make their classroom more student-centered and empowering to all of our students!"

—**A.J. Juliani**, innovation specialist and co-author of *LAUNCH*

"*Shift This!* by Joy Kirr is a treasure of real examples to maximize student engagement for any classroom, no matter the grade or subject area. Through the pages of this book, I felt as though I was a part of Joy's classroom. This uplifting, practical book is a must-read, and I can't wait to implement the ideas in my own school."

—**Beth Houf**, middle school principal and co-author of *Lead Like a PIRATE*

"Education needs to adapt to the changing workforce and learning culture. While many education experts keep shouting to change, many teachers need an example on how to shift the school culture. That's why *Shift This!* is so important. Joy Kirr offers practical advice for teachers to start shifting their classrooms—*now!*"

—**Don Wettrick**, author of *Pure Genius*

"Teachers looking to reboot their teaching practice will find tons of easy-to-implement strategies in *Shift This!* The wisdom Kirr shares comes from an amazing teaching career full of learning and sharing."

—**Kevin Brookhouser**, author of *Code in Every Class* and *The 20Time Project*

"Passionate, innovative educator Joy Kirr penned a book that will lead positive change in classrooms around the world. *Shift This! How to Implement Gradual Change for Massive Impact in Your Classroom* made me feel as if I were sitting on my couch with my favorite cup of coffee chatting with this amazing educator. The conversational style of this book makes each suggestion seem immediately doable, and as I read I find myself becoming more and more energized and inspired with each passing page. As I finish the book, I am encouraged by the change that I am convinced will occur in the classrooms of readers around the world. Master teachers and novices alike should read this energizing and inspirational book."

—**Nancy Vandiver Wahl**, Second Baptist School, Houston, Texas

"As a teacher, I'm always on the lookout for practical ideas and suggestions that are easy to understand and implement in my classroom without *tons* of preparation and *drastic* philosophical changes. *Shift This!*, by Joy Kirr, provides subtle, yet powerful mindset 'shifts' that have the potential to make a *huge* impact on student learning, engagement, and empowerment in every classroom!"

—**Paul Solarz**, fifth grade teacher and author of *Learn Like a Pirate*

SHIFT THIS!

How to
Implement
Gradual
Changes for
MASSIVE
Impact in
Your Classroom

Joy Kirr

SHIFT THIS!

> This book is available at special discounts when purchased in quantity for use as premiums, promotions, fundraising, and educational use. For inquiries and details, contact us: shelley@daveburgessconsulting.com.

Published by Dave Burgess Consulting, Inc.
San Diego, CA
http://daveburgessconsulting.com

Cover Design by Genesis Kohler
Editing and Interior Design by My Writers' Connection

Library of Congress Control Number: 2017940076
Paperback ISBN: 978-1-946444-09-7
Ebook ISBN: 978-1-946444-10-3
First Printing: April 2017

CONTENTS

JOIN THE SHIFT!

shiftthis.weebly.com

1 | The Catalyst

If you don't like it, take it apart and make it right.

—*Navigating Early* by Clare Vanderpool

"**C**an anyone show me how to start a new website?"

"Oooh! I just started one at 'Simple Site.' I can help!" Nicole says. She sits down next to Erin and they work together to amplify Erin's budding business with a new website.

A few desks down, Michael sits lamenting the fact that no one is buying any more fudge from his two-month-old business. Finding out that students cannot sell products at school has put a damper on his enthusiasm. He is stuck this week, not knowing where to go. I see him sitting by himself and head over with a blank sheet of paper. "Write down all of your thoughts, ideas, and hopes," I whisper, placing the paper in front of him. Rather than wait for a response, I walk away to see what Alex and Ben are up to. Hopefully by writing down his thoughts, Michael will be able to take a step back and realize that his project is not doomed.

"Look, Mrs. Kirr, I took Elise's feedback and made the dog's ears pointier!"

"Yeah, and he's distracting me from my reading, Mrs. Kirr!" (said with a smirk upon his face because he'd rather watch Ben draw this week than read on his own). They both have two Genius Hour projects going on at one time: working on getting better at drawing and also at reading. Most of the time Alex reads more at home than at school, and I'm okay with that as long as he's helping others in class instead of hindering their progress. I was glad to see Ben taking the advice from the video we'd watched last week (Austin's Butterfly), asking peers for feedback and making multiple drafts of the same drawing.

"Have either of you finished writing your goal for the next two weeks? How much did you accomplish these past two weeks? What did you decide for the next two? Don't forget, Spring Break is coming up, so you'll actually have three weeks to accomplish this next one."

Alisa walks up and gives me her two-week goal sheets: one from the previous two weeks with her reflection on it and a new one for the next two weeks. I look them over and then hold them close so I don't lose them until I can put them in their proper place. "Thank you, Alisa. I'm happy you decided to reflect using more details this week. I have fewer questions about what your project is." Ben and Alex give me a verbal update before I move on to another student, remembering to drop off Alisa's new goal sheet on the file cabinet and tuck her previous one away. I check out the clock, knowing I'll be announcing time to begin their reflections for their work today with ten minutes left to spare. Many of them have been choosing to do their reflections at home, however, and use the last ten minutes to keep working ... on something they love.

This was a typical Monday in my seventh grade ELA classroom last year: students helping one another, celebrating successes, struggling with decisions and failures, and goofing off a bit as they work together or independently on something they love. I ran around like a wild woman and saw half of my students one-on-one for conferences to check out their progress on their two-week goals. I then checked in with as many of the rest of the class as I could in the time we had left. I never graded, read, or even checked email (unless it was to check for a response a student was waiting for) during this precious hour of time. Nor did I want to.

In a student-centered classroom, we, as teachers, spend our time learning about and helping our students. It can feel as if a thousand things are going on at once and can be difficult to manage, but this type of class is not about what I (or you) can handle. It's all about the students. It's all about what the students are accomplishing and learning during this time. When people from other classes visit, they often ask if there's a teacher in the room. My answer: Heck, yes! There are twenty-six or so teachers in the room at any given time—my students.

Five years ago, I decided to give my students time to learn what *they* wanted to learn. I knew I needed to give some ownership of the week over to the students because what I was doing seemed too rigid and, really, just too much. As the "sage on the stage," I was working harder than the kids, and I knew I needed to let go of some control. I found some ideas on Twitter to help initiate the kind of changes I desired for my class, and the students and I have morphed it into the self-directed learning it is today. I now know I could never go back to the way things used to be. That said, finding a system that works for my students and for me did not happen overnight. Not even close! I continually—to this day—question what it should look like. My motto has become, "Just keep tweaking. Just keep tweaking," as I change how to introduce student-directed learning and keep it going with the same enthusiasm each year.

This hour given to students every week goes by many names: Passion-Driven Learning, Student-Driven Learning, Student-Directed Learning, Self-Directed Learning, Wonder Wednesday, Passion Projects, Innovation Days, 20 Percent Time, Personal Research, Personal Inquiry, and the list goes on. Whatever you call it has to work for you, or it won't work for your students.

My class called this time "Genius Hour."

Giving this class time over to students changed my views on what teaching should look like and has been as much a journey of learning for me as it has been for them. In fact, starting Genius Hour prompted me to begin blogging—so I could ask other teachers for help! In my seventeen years of teaching (at that point), it was the hardest thing I'd tried! That's why I wrote this book. I wanted to share with you the tiny, deliberate shifts that have had a large, positive impact on the way things transpire in my classroom.

Genius Hour is a just a piece of something bigger that all educators are aiming for. We want our students to be lifelong learners, to be successful outside of school, and to explore—and exploit!—their passions so they can have a fulfilling life.

This book is all about small changes and incremental shifts. Ironically, I jumped into Genius Hour. There was nothing subtle about my shift. And once I made the leap, I began to question and alter many other aspects of classroom time. I realize, however, that not everyone wants to jump in with a big splash. And I get it. I've already told you it was hard; there are days I felt like I needed someone to rescue me from the chaos. I've since learned that you don't have to dive in all at once to make huge, positive changes. That's why I want to share the *tiny* shifts you can implement in your class *tomorrow*. Each one can lead to larger and larger shifts (such as implementing Genius-Hour-type learning) throughout the year, or even in subsequent years. We all want classes where our students want to come to learn more. We want a culture of learning. My own class has been transformed as a result of tiny shifts! It *can* be done. It *should* be done—if you want students to enjoy learning and build lifelong learning habits.

You don't have to dive in all at once to make huge, positive changes.

We'll start by looking at aspects of the classroom that are the easiest to tweak. Beginning with the classroom environment, I'll share very simple tweaks. You may have already implemented some of them, such as letting students decorate. From there, we'll move on to shifts that will lead to not-so-easy or I'm-not-quite-ready-yet changes. As we explore these less-subtle shifts, you'll discover that the kinds of changes that may seem to be "too much" now are actually quite feasible and will make a huge difference in your classroom's culture. In subsequent chapters I will address other aspects of teaching, such as classwork, homework, and grading. I will end with student-directed learning, in the hopes that many teachers in all content areas and grade levels will try a version of it. I know it can seem overwhelming. I've been there. I was driven by the reasons behind the shifts—my students.

My main goal with *Shift This!* is that, as I share my journey and the small shifts I've made to promote student-owned, student-led learning in my classroom, you will begin to feel comfortable and confident enough to make shifts, bit by bit, toward creating the kind of classroom culture you've always dreamed of. My hope is for you to discover your own *aha* moments and, perhaps, realize that you never want to go back to the way things were. It's an ongoing process. Every year gets better and better for me and for my students because of the shifts I continue to make. I wish you the same kind of success!

2 Beginnings

Studies have shown that thinking and wondering lead to thoughtful decision-making.

—Furthermore by Tahereh Mafi

It's the first day of school.

Directions for students are on the board. Everything is in its place. I'm anxious. The bell rings for the first of three of my seventh grade ELA classes.

I shake twenty-five hands at the door, welcoming each student, introducing myself, and asking their names. When everyone is in the classroom, I see that the students are sitting on the floor gathered around my mom's rocking chair. The Important Book by Margaret Wise Brown is on the chair, along with my district-issued iPad. I climb over legs and arms to sit in the rocker, wait with a smile, and begin talking quietly. I say something like this: "Before I begin reading our first book of the year, I'm going to ask each of you to take a selfie on my iPad. My plan is to know all your names by the end of the week. Do you think I can do it?" I hear murmurs, or outright blurts, of who-knows-what in response. The iPad gets passed around, and giggles are heard from the start. I continue, "We have only ten minutes, so let's make the best of it by sharing a book." As

I read The Important Book aloud, I ask for responses to see if students agree and what they think of the book. I get my first clue that shows these students have learned how to be compliant. They've learned how to raise their hands to take turns. They've also learned how to give the teacher what they think she wants: affirmations. Yes, they agree with the author. Yes, they can tell me what they enjoy about the illustrations (even though, personally, they're not my favorite). So when I get to the page about the apple, I ask them, "What do you think is the most important thing about an apple? 'The most important thing about an apple is ...'"

"It's juicy!"

"It's crispy!"

"It's for eating!"

"It's to keep you healthy!"

"It's to keep the doctor away!"

"It is red."

I question that student. "Do you really think the most important thing about an apple is that it is red?"

"No."

"Then why did you say so?"

"I think that's what the author will say."

It's a response I get every year, and this is my third clue that these students are used to being compliant. They want to be right. What twelve-year-old doesn't want to be right?

Before I turn the page, we talk about how many picture books have repetition. Why do they repeat certain phrases? What's the point? Who thinks the author will say that it is red? If so, would you agree? I still haven't turned the page. I let them know: "I would not agree. I've eaten my fair share of green apples. I think one of your answers—that it is juicy, or healthy, or for eating—should be the answer."

When I turn the page, most students are confused that the text says, "The most important thing about an apple is that it is round." Those who are upset are the ones who will be looking for As on their report cards; this answer did not fit the pattern. This answer does not make sense to them. Some students are disappointed that the author chose this time to be contradictory. "Round?!" They believe she should have written one of the other ideas we shared. I know that these are the students who will lead the way during the next few months as we figure out how to shift our middle school classroom from teacher-led to student-driven.

At this point, I stop reading the book, explain that I don't like the book's answer, and as an informed reader, I don't have to agree with authors. I inform students that this year, we'll be asking questions so we can find out more information. We'll be questioning authors, questioning one another, and even questioning teachers. I let them know right off the bat that if they don't think a lesson is relevant, they can politely challenge me. If I cannot answer, I'll reconsider the lesson; being inquisitive and listening to responses is how we will learn together.

QUESTIONS FOR THE READER

» What did you like and not like about this quick lesson?

» How do you start your first ten minutes with students on the first day of the school year?

» If you are a veteran teacher, how has your teaching changed over the past ten or twenty years?

» If you are a new teacher, how do you imagine your teaching will change in the next ten or twenty years?

MY FIRST FOURTEEN YEARS

My teaching career has been a series of shifts—in mindset, practice, and experience. During my first seven years, I served as an itinerant teacher in the "wilds" of McHenry County, Illinois. My students were children who were deaf or hard-of-hearing, and they ranged in age from three to eighteen. Many of these students needed me to help them read. Since I hadn't really learned how to teach reading in my undergrad courses, I went back to school to earn my master's degree in reading. I spent the next seven years as the reading specialist at my current school. My specific role in this position fluctuated as necessary—sometimes I taught classes on a regular basis, sometimes I pulled students out of class for one-on-one help, and sometimes I co-taught the class. I visited social studies, science, reading, language arts, and even math middle school classes during these seven years.

I also became the ELA (English Language Arts) department head and became National Board Certified. Despite my education and experience, I had a teacher tell me, "You don't know what we're going through. You're not in the classroom." She was right. I didn't know the pressures of being in one classroom, with a curriculum I was supposed to cover day-in and day-out. How hard could it be? It had to be easier than what I was doing at the time. My fifteenth year, I found out when I transitioned into a seventh-grade ELA position. It was our school's inaugural year of the ELA "block" (reading and writing taught by the same teacher for eighty-minute increments), and I wanted *in*. I'd only be teaching *three* classes each day—full of reading and writing. Finally, all the children's books I'd been collecting for fourteen years would have a home—in the hands of my students.

YEAR FIFTEEN

I was thrilled that I was going to have my own classroom. My name would be on the wall outside the door, and I would finally be called a "real teacher." I was even going to be on a team at the middle school level! Each team consisted of two ELA teachers, one math, one P.E./health, one science, one social studies, and one resource (special education) teacher. We would meet every day for one period (team time) to talk about students, curricula, and activities. (Our school currently has two teams per grade. In this book I may refer to "team members" and "department members." There are four ELA department members at each grade, with two on each team. We also have an advanced ELA teacher.)

That summer I bought new clothes (no, this lateral shift did not come with a raise), because I wanted new outfits to go along with my new title. At home, I got out the basal and the workbooks, read the books we were going to teach, took copious notes about the vocabulary and characters, and started copying grammar worksheets. I called my coworker and set a date to plan the first few weeks. Of course, I'd already planned the bulletin boards and bought the decorations as well as magnets for the whiteboard. (I even had an overhead projector!) I carefully arranged my room and figured out the perfect seating arrangement. I had my plans and worksheet originals ready to fill up the four-drawer filing cabinet well before the first day of school. Luckily for me, I was a middle-school reading freak, so I could fill the sparse shelving with books for this level. The oldies-but-goodies were all labeled with my name in the upper left of the inside cover, organized by author's last name, and lined up straight as rods. I was ready to rock and roll!

Halfway through the year, I started questioning all sorts of things about the room I'd so carefully planned and arranged:

- How could I move the tables and chairs so that students participated more?

- Why don't some kids turn in assignments?

- Why do I have so much to grade all the time?

- Why was I spending more time creating rubrics and grading than the kids were spending on the assignments?

- What would happen to a student's grade if she didn't get the big project due on the last day of the quarter in on time?

- How could I get my students to love grammar when I didn't love it myself?

- Why did they have to memorize how old each character was in *The Outsiders* when I couldn't remember either?

- How can I get my kids to read the books on the shelves?

- Why don't they follow the clues from the posters?

Halfway through the year, I started questioning all sorts of things about the room I'd so carefully planned and arranged.

Sometimes, my students gave *me* ideas: "Why don't you create a checkmark and put it on the board when someone figures out the brainteaser for the day?"

"Can I sit at that empty table so I can focus better today?"

"Can we have time to do the homework in class?"

"Can we check out the laptops to write instead of writing in our notebooks?"

I had more questions and ideas in my mind than in any year prior. It was like my very first year of teaching all over again. I knew diddly-squat about how to teach middle schoolers. All I knew were worksheets, grading, and compliance. My own experiences in school were all I had to draw upon—as is the case with most teachers.

YEAR TWENTY-TWO (PRESENT DAY)

The tables now have casters that roll and most are painted with whiteboard paint. One bulletin board is covered with student-chosen decorations and articles. More bookshelves (courtesy of my husband's craftsmanship) are filled with books (from many book sales and gift cards) organized by genre. On the board are names of the students who are in charge of the three classroom iPads this week. Also on the board is the homework, "Read for at least twenty minutes." Small magnets with each student's name written on them are scattered all over the board. A "student station" has replaced the teacher's desk.

Many activities we do look like chaos to an outsider. In all honesty, it does get quite messy; I have yet to assign the job of class custodian. Next year, for sure …

I began writing this book during my twentieth year because I felt a need to share how (and why) I've created the shift into teaching the way I believe we are supposed to be teaching—with a focus on children first and content second. Putting my ego aside and starting to cater to the students' needs made all the difference. I realized that my teaching is not all about me and what I do during class. It's all about the students and what *they* do during class. It's about the choices (or lack thereof) students have.

With these changes come great trust and a classroom culture that will surprise you. No, these changes do not take the world off your shoulders, but they do make the world a brighter place. In the following chapters, you'll learn about the tiny changes that can create seismic shifts, and you'll see that these changes are, indeed, feasible for you. Once you shift your teaching or your classroom environment that slightest bit, you'll want more of what comes with the shift. What comes with it? Student buy-in! Student buy-in means student engagement, which equals more student learning—of YOUR content. It's addicting!

With this being said, I aspire to continue to grow as a teacher. I used to have what Carol Dweck calls a "fixed mindset." I thought I was either a good teacher or a bad teacher, and that's how it would stay. I have since developed much more of a "growth mindset." My students and I constantly try out new ideas and then we reflect on them. I hope to find emails and comments from readers on my blog posts that challenge my thinking, and/or add ideas for us to try. Striving for mastery in my teaching is what keeps me motivated. I'll always want to do what's best for my students each day. I want to get better and better every year. I don't think you'd be reading this if you didn't feel the same. Join me in making small shifts that will make your classroom one that students—and you—will never forget. Commit to improving year after year, starting today.

REFLECTION AND CALL TO ACTION

With what aspect(s) of your teaching do you struggle? Write down, right here, what you would most like guidance with. Next, write down who you can go to for advice or mentorship. Finally, on your to-do list, make a note to contact that person and begin the discussion.

_____

_____

_____

_____

_____

_____

3 | Questions

Asking why is the way to wisdom.

—*Lots of Candles, Plenty of Cake* by Anna Quindlen

I don't understand why I'm doing more work than the kids. How can they turn in their quarterly book project without even reading the book and STILL get an A? We really need to revise the rubric—again.

Then there's the test for S.E. Hinton's The Outsiders. *Why is it fifty questions? Why do the kids have to know every character's age? Do they really have to be able to explain what "madras" means? Can't we just give them the slang words so they understand the story better, and then focus on the words they do not understand while they're reading?*

One great aspect of education is that teachers are in a position to change what they do in the classroom. Why change if things are going well? Um … why not? Our kids are changing, and we need to change alongside them. It's time (if you haven't already) to start reflecting on what you're doing (or not doing) in the classroom. It's time to ask more WHY questions and, perhaps more importantly, HOW over and over again.

The questions at the opening of this chapter were a few I asked during my first year in the seventh grade ELA classroom. I knew something had to change, yet I knew my coworkers had been doing these things for many years by the time I arrived. Who was I to know what's right? Who was I to upset the apple cart? Although we got off to a great start, my coworkers and I slowly grew apart during my first year in this position. I wanted—no, I *needed*—change in order to be happy.

Pause for a moment and think about what you feel needs to be changed in your classroom or school environment. Perhaps you notice the need most when you're at home; is something from school taking over too much of your home life? What is the problem? What is wrong? Until you figure out what's wrong it will be impossible to solve the issue.

> Until you figure out what's wrong it will be impossible to solve the issue.

Listed below are more questions I (and my fellow teachers) have asked during the past five years of shifting the classroom.

QUESTIONS REGARDING STUDENTS

> » Why do I have to repeat myself so often?
>
> » Why can't they follow directions?
>
> » Why aren't they checking out books?
>
> » Why don't they like to read?
>
> » Why won't they stop playing with each other's hair?
>
> » Why are they talking when they're supposed to be listening?
>
> » Why can't they tell I'm upset and I mean what I say?

» Why won't they revise their papers?

» Why don't they turn in their homework on time ... or at all?

» Why don't they like me?

» Why do they keep pushing my buttons?

» Why are they late to class?

» Why do they have to take a bathroom break each day in my class?

» Why aren't they paying attention?

» Why do they ask me questions I've already answered?

» Why don't they care?

QUESTIONS REGARDING MY PRACTICES

» Why do I have to decorate the bulletin boards when the students don't even look at them?

» Why are we giving huge tests for books with only 224 pages?

» Why do we go over every chapter after students are supposed to read it on their own?

» Do they even *need* to read them if we go over it each day?

» Why am I spending so much time (every year) revising rubrics that the kids can seemingly ace without doing any real work?

» Why do we spend eight weeks reading one novel?

» Why can't we just enjoy reading without taking a quiz or test on it?

Learn why high school students don't read what's assigned in class: **tinyurl.com/ShiftHSReaders**.

QUESTIONS FROM TEACHERS

» What will administration think?

» What will the parents think?

» Do I have to grade everything?

» Do I have to give homework every night?

» Do I have to offer re-dos if that means they won't try the first time around?

THE "HOW" QUESTIONS REGARDING PRODUCTIVITY

» How can I make a warm-up activity that is engaging *and* educational?

» How can I teach vocabulary without asking students to create flash cards?

» Can I find a way for students to choose the words they need to know?

» How can I provide students with more time to express all their thoughts and ideas?

» How can I get rid of all these worksheets but still get the ideas across to students?

» How can I not simply make a worksheet digital and instead create an interactive activity?

» How can I grade less?

» How can I give a test where students *can* use the resources (text and notes) if they need them?

» How can I get students reading more, and how can I hold them accountable?

» How can my students be more active learners in class?

» How can my students be more engaged with the curriculum?

» How can I empower my students?

That's quite a list, and I have a notebook full of even more of them! These questions led me to begin transforming our ELA class. And I knew I had to start with the "HOW" questions.

During my second year in this position, I was given the opportunity to hear Ewan McIntosh speak at a workshop in Bloomfield Hills, Michigan. I attended the workshop with a group of twenty or so teachers and administrators. I didn't have a clue who this innovator was, but he asked a question that turned my 2011–2012 year on its head:

> *What's a problem you see in your school or classroom, and how can you begin solving it today?*

It didn't take me long to decide what issue I would work on: independent reading. Our sixth, seventh, and eighth graders referred to this as quarterly book projects. Seriously? Here's some background: Each quarter, our seventh graders were expected to read one book (first quarter—students' choice, second quarter—teachers chose a genre, third quarter—biography/autobiography or memoir, fourth quarter—students' choice). We had projects lined up for them to do too. One was a CD cover (extra credit given if you actually put the songs on a CD!) that had songs relating to the conflict, a character, and an important scene in the book. Another was a scrapbook page that depicted the life of the person about whom they were reading. The projects made me sick, even though I expressed great interest in them for the students' sake. Everything was so structured, and *any* student could receive an A by reading the summary of the book online and explicitly following directions.

My questions came back to the forefront:

> » Where is the choice built into this project?
>
> » Why do the teachers decide what students should do to show they are reading?
>
> » Why do students have to make a plot diagram for every story?
>
> » Why are we only expecting them to read four books a year??
>
> » Why do I work harder on the rubric than they do on the actual project?
>
> » HOW can I encourage students to read MORE?

That day, February 12, 2012, my world changed. I sat down with Jen Smith (a teacher from another local middle school, edtechsmith. blogspot.com), and we came up with a plan. This plan is how I began Genius Hour reading and research with my students.

Also on this day, I started to understand the value of Twitter. Our principal had encouraged us to set up an account the August prior, and I did, but I had no clue how using Twitter could help me as an educator. (It would only be a distraction; of that I was sure.) This workshop had its own hashtag, and we were asked to tweet our notes, quotes, and new ideas to it—even after the workshop ended. I learned how to use Twitter that day, from the basics of replying to people to using a hashtag to organize tweets. More importantly, I learned how to contribute ideas and how to stay connected with these passionate teachers. For those of you who use Twitter regularly, you can probably guess what happened during the next couple of years. For those of you who haven't dipped your toes in yet—you're in for a transformation of your own classroom when you do. Twitter will allow you to connect with and learn from experts around the world. (You'll learn about how you can shift a few minutes of your day toward this amazing, ongoing learning opportunity in the chapter on social media.)

Are you ready to make some shifts in your classroom? Are you ready to let students own more of the learning, become more engaged in your lessons, and help run the class themselves? Are you ready for your plans to be more student-driven? Then start with the same question:

What's a problem you see in your school or classroom, and how can you begin solving it today?

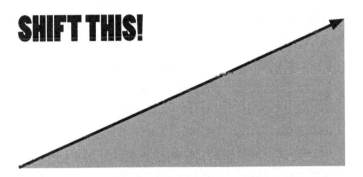

Once you figure out the questions you want to answer, it's time to start shifting your teaching. Throughout this book, you'll find sliding scales for shifting portions of your day. Each scale will begin with small shifts any teacher should be able to do in his or her classroom. These are small shifts that will let your students know that you care about their opinions or that you trust them with choices. These are small shifts that *just make sense*. There will be subsequent shifts after this small beginning, and with each shift, you will empower your students further. Every time you see this graphic, it gives you a glimpse into what you can do immediately to shift the learning to your students. The goal is to shift from student engagement to student empowerment.

Suppose for a moment you teach ELA. Let's see what your independent reading could look like with a shift or two …

Shift A: Instead of choosing the types of books students are required to choose, let them choose their own genres, authors, and types of reading (book, newspaper, magazine, blogs).

Shift B: Instead of giving students a date when they need to share their reading with you, let them choose which date they'd like to share with the class. Of course you can give the parameters of weeks in which they should share. A personal log of some sort could assist them in figuring out what books are worth sharing with a larger audience.

Shift C: Let students choose HOW they will share what they're reading. This can be as informal (as we do in "real life") as leading a conversation with the class, to as formal as a practiced speech with visuals to share. How about a video book trailer or advertisement?

Shift D: You may still be using rubrics at this point. It's time to let them go, and have students self-assess their reading and/or their sharing. If you decide to have them assess their own reading, you could go the route of how much reading they're doing each quarter, how much effort they put into their choice of reading, or effort applied to finding time to read independently. If you let them assess their presentation, stick to the basics—maintaining an appropriate volume, keeping the audience engaged, and sharing why they enjoyed what they read. Here's a form we now use for instant feedback when students share books: tinyurl.com/FeedbackBookShare.

Shift E: It's time to let the self-reflections and assessments be just that. Do not attach a grade to this reading or sharing. Do real readers give themselves grades? Instead of a grade, challenge your students to read __ books a year, or to read __ books in each genre. Challenge them to read twenty minutes per day or to create their *own* challenge. The learning is in the reflection and the action that your students will take based on this reflection.

This sample shift is the tip of the iceberg. I'm excited for you to start making some shifts as you begin exploring the answers to your own reflection questions! These shifts will transform the culture of your classroom into one of respect and trust. Your students will be even more motivated to learn as a result.

REFLECTION AND CALL TO ACTION

» What questions do you have about your class?

» It's time for you to consider—and write down—your questions.

» What do you feel is just not right in your classroom?

» Ask your WHY questions, then transform them into HOW questions.

» Write those HOW questions here so you can be proactive in answering them.

_____

_____

_____

_____

_____

_____

_____

_____

_____

4 Classroom Environment

Everything is worth a second glance.

—*A Work in Progress* by Connor Franta

"*W*hat's with the masking tape line by your desk?" someone asks at the beginning of a team meeting.

Another responds, "The other day, I saw kids going to my desk and taking the tape without asking. Then I saw another one looking through my desk drawers!"

Ooops ... I cringe a bit as I realize this exchange is a direct result of my own classroom shift. I need to talk to my students today and let them know that not every desk is a "student station" like ours in room 239.

"Um, it's probably a little bit my fault," I butt in. "My desk this year is not my desk anymore. It's our 'student station,' so all the supplies are theirs, and they can even sit there if they'd like. Sorry."

Since overhearing that conversation a few years ago, I make sure my students know that our room is the *only* room with a student station in it, unless they hear otherwise from another teacher. The other teachers have more traditional desks—mine just happens to be the filing cabinet. This small shift is one I have benefitted from maybe even more than the students.

Giving up one's desk can be a difficult shift for most teachers, so let's start with something a little easier. First, take a look at the questions below that led me to shift the classroom environment. I skipped the questions that start with "Why"—I knew the reason for changing the classroom environment was to make students feel welcome. I wanted students to *want* to be in our classroom. I wanted them to know it was *ours*, and not solely *mine*. I went right to the HOW.

» How can I make our class more inviting?

» How can I make the seating more comfortable?

» How can I encourage independent, pair, and group work, as well as whole-class discussions?

» How can I encourage more student interest in my particular subject in this room?

» How can I help other staff feel comfortable using my room?

» How can I make my room not just about reading and writing, since other teachers use this room?

» How can I give the resource teacher room for her supplies for when she's using the room for her class?

» How can I share classroom supplies with the teachers who use this room?

» How can I share classroom supplies with students—without having them ask me about them every day?

» How can I share our agenda, classwork, assignments, project dates, reflections, and class celebrations with students ... and also with parents?

My classroom isn't solely mine. It is very much my students' environment. Beyond that, it is each teacher's and student's classroom. Perhaps my perspective comes from having been an itinerant teacher without a classroom. I used to drive to five schools a day on average. I pulled students out of their classrooms and into the hallway, a closet, the cafeteria, the band room. I've been the teacher who says to students, "Let's find a space to use today," and searched for five precious instructional minutes to find a space that wasn't being used at the time. I've asked teachers during their planning time, "Can we use your room?" Most of the time, my request was granted. Sometimes the teacher even went to work in the copy room or lounge so we could use their space. Having spent fourteen years trying to find a room in which to work, it is my belief that the classrooms belong to the *students*, and not solely the teachers. My advice to all classroom teachers is to treat "visiting" teachers with respect. In turn they'll treat the room and its contents with respect.

Now that I've had a designated room for a few years, I realize the importance of how it is set up. The young minds that walk into room 239 (what I used to call "my room") know from day one (I hope!) that it is *their* room. They will be the interior designers, the custodians, and the reporters. And, of course, we'll provide room for anyone else who needs room to work! Let's talk about the small shifts.

SHIFT YOUR WALLS

» What do the walls of your classroom look like?

» What message are you sending to students based on what you have on your walls?

» How can you use the wall space you have to let students know they matter and are included in the decisions in the classroom?

Wall space is limited in my classroom. On one wall, a row of windows (for which I'm grateful) lets light into the classroom. Another set of windows to the hallway line the upper portion of the room along the opposite wall. Storage shelves and a long narrow bulletin board fill a third of the space under those windows. In the front of the room is the white board and a small set of shelves, and the back wall holds shelves of books (it used to be another bulletin board). Whatever wall space you do have, the shifts below will help you and your students make the most of them.

FIND YOUR ARTISTS!

Try to start the year with blank walls. This can feel so scary when everyone else in the school is decorating the days before the school year begins. You may be wondering, *What will the parents think when they come in for Parent Night or Open House? What are the benefits, if any? Why blank walls? Why??* Because it leaves the room open to possibilities! Not only does leaving your walls blank lessen your prep time at the beginning of the year, it also lets students wonder what this class will be like. Let them know it is all about *them*.

During the first few weeks of school, let the students decorate the bulletin boards. Sure, you can provide some decorations, but emphasize that you'd like *them* to do the decorating, as it is *their* room. They might not take any initiative to do this on their own (they have probably never been asked to do this before!), so consider making it a "job" or "responsibility" in your room. Change out who does this job every month or season. You could even create a decorating club! Your decorators may want (or need) to come in during lunch or before or after school to plan and execute their decorations.

UNLEASH CREATIVITY!

The second shift is literally close by. They've decorated the bulletin boards, so now it's time to let them decorate the rest of the space. They can create masterpieces, doodles, lessons learned, advertisements, articles, websites, book recommendations, stories written, QR codes ... the list is endless. Ask them what they'd like to display! What else can be taken care of by the students around your four walls? The agenda or homework written on the front board, the goal for the day or week, and the question of the day can all be taken care of by *students*—with a little help or organization from you. Typical concrete block walls are just begging for artwork, so be ready when students ask, "Can we paint on the walls?" That is a question to pose to your administration. You could bolster your request by volunteering to paint over it next year if needed. Find your residing student artists and let them use their talents!

Note: I am by no means saying don't decorate your room at all! I'm just asking you to leave some of it (most of it!) up to the students. I found one of my favorite decorations, thanks to a photo Kimberly Hurd Horst (@khurdhorst on Twitter) shared with me. I put a huge branch (my husband helps me find and pack in the car) in the corner of the room and make it look like it is coming out of the corner walls. Students decorate the branch with poetry. Suddenly, it's a "Poet Tree!" The kids love adding their words and decorations to our Poet Tree. Many of your own decorations can be embellished by your students. Let them make the classroom theirs.

ASK A QUESTION

One shift that has helped me get to know my students and simultaneously let them know their opinion counts, is the "question of the day." After seeing the idea posted by a teacher on Twitter, I modified it to work for us. I have four periods a day with students in the room: homeroom, block 2/4, block 5/6, and block 8/9. Every day, I post a question on the front board. It might be on scratch paper, hanging by a clip or a magnet, or simply written on the board (although those tend to get erased/altered). The question has to be one in which there is a choice for an answer. This could be a yes/no answer, an answer on a scale of some sort (1 to 10, 7 p.m. to 3 a.m., "not so much" to "of course!"), or a multiple choice answer. You can bet that a student will add another choice if none of them apply to him or her.

The original goals for this question of the day were twofold: give students something to do when they first walk in, and see who is absent at a glance. To use the question to check attendance, each student's name or photo must be a separate entry. For our classroom, I made magnets with each student's name using an 8.5" x 11" sheet of magnet that can go through the printer. I create a doc that lists students' names in four columns and eleven rows so that I get eighty-eight name magnets from one sheet. This past year, I color coordinated the magnets by class period. Once students move their magnets to answer the question, I can see who is absent, or who simply didn't answer the question. (I don't force an answer, but if they do not move their name it gives me an opportunity to talk with that student one-on-one.) I've seen similar ideas with smaller classes that use student photos in hanging charts, students who write their names under their choice, and Popsicle® sticks with names in cups under the choices for the day.

You can use the question of the day for educational purposes, such as organizing students into groups, or asking their opinion on the lesson from the day prior. You can use it to stress a point or give a reminder, such as "How many hours of sleep did you get last night?" during the week of state testing. The question "What do you normally have for breakfast?" (cereal, pancakes/waffles, bread, meat, eggs, nothing) alerts you to who is not eating in the morning. On Mondays, the question "How was your weekend?" with a scale below it alerts you to who may not be paying attention that day due to some unfortunate event over the weekend. You can also teach students to read the questions carefully by choosing specific wording: Instead of "Who do you WANT to win?" try "Who do you PREDICT will win?" (This phrasing also helps alleviate hard feelings and doesn't pit students against one another.) Or use the question of the day to introduce new vocabulary.

> ## So Many Possibilities!
> Check out this link to see some of the questions
> I have collected through the years. It's an ever-
> evolving list, thanks to students' ideas.
> **shiftthis.weebly.com/question-of-the-day.html**

This small shift on one of our classroom walls is a hit with the kids and can be very useful to you as well. The next shift? Have students create the questions, put them up, and move the magnets back to their starting place! One student at the end of your day will often ask to take on this role, while other students will wonder, "What's the question for tomorrow?"

BUILD TRUST BY PROVIDING A SIMPLE FREEDOM

How many times do you have to ask another person if you can use the restroom? Most likely, your answer is zero. You are able to leave meetings with a simple, "Excuse me." Students should learn this art as well. Using the toilet is a right, not a privilege. But the fact that students are *still* asking me if they can use the restroom (even though we've had the sign-out sheet up all year!) makes me think they're still required to ask for permission in other classes.

I know your concerns. You're wondering whether students will abuse this freedom. That's why we have a sign-out sheet hanging on a clipboard on the wall in our classroom. It serves as a history of students who need to leave. I keep the older sheets and quickly tally who has left (and how many times) every four weeks. If you ever need to have a conversation to address an issue about leaving too frequently, the sheets will support your concern. But I've found that the need for such conversations is rare.

Imagine a classroom environment that is not disrupted by students asking if they can use the facilities. Imagine the respect students will feel if they can leave without the embarrassment of asking. One simple addition of a clipboard to the classroom could build trust and understanding in the environment.

SHIFT YOUR FURNITURE

» How can I make our seating more comfortable?

» How can I be sure all students can see and hear all lessons and all other students?

» How does our seating arrangement help encourage learning?

» How does our seating arrangement encourage individual, pair, and group work?

» How can I help that active student who just can't sit?

Sharing Spaces

Do you have students who need to fidget in order to concentrate? Dedicate one drawer in a desk or file cabinet for sensory fidget toys. My co-teacher, Yvette Rehberger, teaches a class in our room at the end of the day. I know it is not *my* room, so I cleaned out one drawer in the four-drawer file cabinet for her supplies. She immediately turned it over to the kids. It holds fidget toys and even a Chromebook they can use.

Consider giving over some of what you deem "your space" to the kids. If students have their own fidget toys and are being distracted by them instead of using them to get focused, find a piece of furniture where you can put the toys during the day. This should be in view of the child, so he knows it is "safe"—not "lost forever"—and then he is responsible to pick it up himself when class is over.

Get Seated... or Not.

Blue plastic chairs. Have you ever sat in one for six or seven hours a day? I don't mind sitting when I'm in for a long day. When we have professional development and I'm sitting in those chairs all day, however, my back aches by the time I'm heading home. What's it like to sit in one of those chairs if you don't even *like* to sit?!

Seating Shift 1: Let students sit on the floor. I've gotten chair cushions at Goodwill for $3 each. (I take one with me when I'm asked to sit in the student chairs all day!) When the stuffing starts to come out, get out the needle and thread and hand it to a student. Seriously. Mending is a life skill!

Seating Shift 2: Watch for inexpensive furniture at resale shops and garage sales. Our classroom has two of those big cushions that have a back and "arms," and a couple of swivel chairs. I've also gotten small bleacher seats at Goodwill. And that rocking chair the students gather around on the first day of school? It stays in the room all year. Once the kids learn that my mom rocked me in that chair as a child, they treat it with respect. Sturdy bar stool for $5.00? Sold. New fabric with your school's colors? Of course! Get creative! It's totally great to have a hodgepodge of furniture. The kids will thank you for the comfy seating and will move each piece around constantly to share with one another (or steal for themselves). If a student has trouble sharing, you may want to implement a monthly chart with the "fun" chair options where students mark off their own name once they've used that seat.

Tables or Desks?

Some teachers don't have an option regarding whether they have tables or desks in their classrooms; the decision has already been made for them. It's that way for me as well. Our classroom has large, heavy tables that have been customized (optimized!) for student use. One year, our curriculum and instruction director told me she'd help in any way to allow changes in my classroom. I immediately said, "Wheels. I want wheels," thinking that it wouldn't happen. The next school year, thanks to my principal, I came back to find casters on the bottoms of our tables! Teachers who are new to our room are shocked when they lean against a table and it moves (theirs don't!), but I love the versatility.

Where Do I Get the Money for That?!

Furniture isn't cheap. If your school doesn't have the budget for the kinds of changes you'd like to make, one of your best options can be grants. Some grants are specifically for certain kinds of furniture, and you have just as much chance of getting these grants as anyone. (One year I applied for and received yoga balls—they were great but sadly only lasted one year. How surprising it was when they'd suddenly expel all the air and dump the child onto the floor!) I write a grant for some form of furniture every other year or so. It can't hurt to ask!

With our movable tables, I have twenty different kinds of seating arrangements that fit the room (see them here: tinyurl.com/ ShiftSeatingArrangements). In many classrooms, the focus is on the whiteboard, but in our classroom, the lessons are not about what's projected in the front of the room. We change the arrangement every few weeks, and sometimes a couple times a day, depending on our needs. To keep the process of rearranging from being a distraction (and being left up to me), I have the students practice moving the tables and chairs, often timing them to see how efficient they can be. They like it when I record the time and see if they can beat it (or, better yet, beat the time of another class) the next time.

Another thing that makes twelve of my fifteen tables special was the result of another shift: whiteboard paint. This paint isn't the cheapest, but I acquired it by applying for and receiving a grant through our local district. (Not all students liked the paint, so we did not paint them all.)

You can ask students to bring their own whiteboard markers and keep a few on hand, along with small rags for erasers. If there are days you do not want students using the whiteboard markers on the tables, set up a system so they know ahead of time. For example, I've used a simple system of different colored paper squares on the board at the front of the room. Green = go ahead and use the markers! Yellow = only use the markers for lesson-related activities. Red = No markers today.

The Power of Choice

Okay, okay. You've got no money to spend and no grants to apply for, but you still want to make the huge, heavy tables and uncomfortable chairs work for your students. One more shift in seating is related to the young people in your room. A question that led me to this shift was, "Would I enjoy someone telling me where to sit (and who to sit near) every day?" My answer: Absolutely not. If I were a student, I know there would be some days I'd want to sit by the door, some days by the window, some days by the vent (that always has cold air blowing out of it), some days in the front, some days in the back, some days with people I know, and some days I'd like to be alone.

How did I learn how to choose my own seat? I've had a lot of practice. A big shift that many teachers still aren't comfortable with is to allow students to practice choice in *where* they sit. This means no fixed seating chart. You can have a discussion first on what will happen if they cannot concentrate in their "new" seats. Let them know that you're invested in their learning and want them to make good decisions, so you're allowing them to practice choosing to sit where they can best listen and work. Setting parameters such as "groups of four or fewer boys or girls" will help initially with large groups that flock together. Ask students to reflect on how they are working together. Confer with them so they can figure out what it is that is hindering or helping them work or focus. That kind of reflection will help them make wiser seating choices.

Of course, you can always step in and let some students know that you'll be making the decision for them that day if it seems they can't find a good balance of sitting by friends and focusing on class work at the same time … *yet*. Include the word "yet," so they know they can still grow and work on this skill. Have another conversation with them afterwards, reflecting on the change in seating.

One way to shift slowly toward this student choice is to create a seating chart but allow students to choose their own seat on certain days (every Tuesday and Thursday, for example) or during certain activities (such as independent reading or writing). This allows some freedom of choice, but you'll still have a seating chart available when a substitute teacher covers your class.

SHIFT TOWARD MUSIC

» How can I incorporate music into my lessons?

» What types of music are students listening to that we can actually listen to in class (and are appropriate)?

» What ARE students listening to these days?

Share a Song

Music can heal. Music can inspire. Music can make us move. Let's use it more to our advantage. Let's use it to help us heal, be inspired, and shake off worry. If you don't already use music in your classroom, your first shift can be to find a song that you love, and share it. Simply play it as students are coming into your class. As soon as you do this, students will want to share their own songs. Great! Take song requests! Put out a clipboard with a piece of paper on it for students' song suggestions. Be sure to listen to the songs (and/or look up the lyrics) before you play them for the class. You will now know what students are listening to, and, most importantly, students will know you will listen to them and value their opinions and interests.

Create a Playlist

What's next? You could use song suggestions to create a big shift right away. Since it's all about the students, create a Google Form that allows students to choose music for different times of the day—writing, creative work, break, etc. Your students will most likely come up with times that you haven't thought of yet. The Google Form will allow you to keep track and refer back to songs throughout the year.

Students' song submissions can lead to great one-on-one discussions as to why a song may not be an appropriate choice for the class (or the individual student, for that matter!). Sometimes children don't realize what's in the songs, or what certain phrases mean. Depending on the age of the child and the song's meaning, you'll need to use your judgment as to whether to have a conversation about the song with students. Don't let the possibility of a "bad" song scare you away from letting students choose music in your classroom! Most children will suggest very appropriate songs, and you'd be surprised how many will want to hear Sebastian the Crab sing "Under the Sea"! Remember, you'll be checking out the songs for yourself before playing them for the class, so while you're relying on their input, you still have control over the final playlist. Every year, I'm surprised at the songs my students know and love. Believe it or not, the Beatles always make an appearance!

Level Up!

Step up the way you incorporate music in your classroom by including an element of "gamification." In an educational setting, gamification is the practice of applying game-design thinking to non-game situations, such as a lesson, subject, or the classroom atmosphere. I have used this technique at a beginner level by allowing students to "win" the privilege to choose the music (or their seats, or ask the question of the day, etc.). They earn points by completing activities throughout the week, month, or grading period and then exchange the points for songs. Gamification works because it keeps students engaged in the work at hand, and they can see progress with the privileges earned.

SHIFT THE TEACHER SPACE

» What message does the top of your desk send to students?

» What message does the placement of your desk in the room send to students?

» How can you make the most of this space?

» How can you make this space more useful to you and your students?

Eliminate Barriers

The first shift to a more student-centered classroom regarding *your* space would be to find a spot in the room that helps make you more available to students. Look at the room from the students' perspective. When they come to speak to you (assuming you ever get a chance to sit at your desk), do they see a barrier between them and you? Can they stand or sit next to you when they ask you a question or share a concern? Can they have a private conversation with you without the other students overhearing? Check out the angle of your desk. When you sit there, are you boxing yourself in, ensuring you have your own space, or is the desk up against a wall, allowing the students more space? How much space do you need in order to be comfortable during your day? The more space you can give to students, the more you'll be sending students the message that they matter.

Create a Student Station

Shifting the physical position of the teacher's desk really makes a difference in the classroom environment. Once you're comfortable with this physical shift, and believe students will be comfortable with it as well, consider the physical supplies on your desk. Are some supplies hidden away because you're afraid of losing them to students, or to another teacher? Are you worried your stapler will break (again) if someone uses it? And yet ... are you asking students to use these supplies throughout your day to accomplish certain activities or tasks? Do you want students to show some creativity in their work? If you teach elementary school, you've probably got bins of supplies for students to use that are not housed on your desk. If you don't have this space for students, consider this shift—letting students use the supplies—anytime. Making a set space for supplies in the room will make your day and your students' day more manageable.

Once I shifted "my desk" over to the students, and began calling it the "student station," they were at once confused, excited, and hesitant. I never sit at this desk while students are in the room. In fact, I encourage students to sit there when they want a different workspace. All of the supplies in this desk are for student (and teacher) use. Supplies are on and under a shoe shelf (great garage sale find) on top of the desk, and also in the drawers. I had previously labeled one drawer as "Ask the teacher before using these supplies," but it didn't work. I needed to give *every* drawer to the students for the supplies to be used effectively. The desk is up against a wall, allowing more shelves if needed, and has easy access to drawers full of supplies. If you do not feel you can hand over your desk to the students, consider creating a space all their own for supplies they can use when needed. Either way, be sure students know to respect the supplies. Make sure they're aware that these supplies need to last all year. Once given the responsibility, they (usually) take it seriously and keep one another accountable.

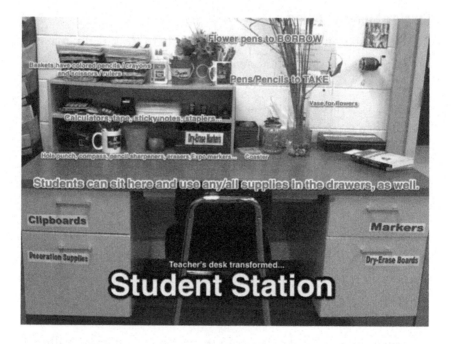

Teacher's desk transformed...
Student Station

Yes, the staplers break. I ask students to try to fix them, or I fix them myself, or I ask another teacher or my husband to see if they can fix it. Yes, I run out of tape—a *lot*. Sometimes I'll wait for a week (or two) before putting out another roll of tape. Students miraculously find ways to cope without tape! When the tape magically appears once again, I don't make a big deal out of it, and neither do the kids. The role of monitoring the tape usage subtly shifts to the students—they call each other out if one is using "too much." I don't fret over the tape or staplers much anymore. I also don't have to tell students where anything is. They look through the student station if they can't find something. As naturally curious creatures, they will find what they're looking for, and I don't have to stop what I'm doing to direct them. The responsibility to take initiative is back where it belongs: on the students. They accept this responsibility gladly and enjoy using the supplies without having to ask. Some days I'll see a student simply looking at everything and taking inventory for future use. And since the students aren't waiting on me to find or pass out supplies, independent and group work is more productive and efficient.

> ## The responsibility to take initiative is back where it belongs: on the students.

If (or *when*) you make this shift, where will you put your work? Where will you sit and work? How can you give your desk over to students and still work productively? Those are questions you'll have to ask and answer. But I promise it's worth the effort and minor inconvenience. At present, my personal supplies and files are stashed in (and on) a four-drawer file cabinet in one corner of the room and on a shelf along the wall adjacent to the file cabinet. If something doesn't fit in or on top of this file cabinet, it goes in the circular file. Not using a desk actually keeps me more organized than I was prior to making my desk the student station. The pile of papers on top of the file cabinet can only get so high before I can't see the top of it anymore and need to file items away. As for where I do my work, it's often at a student table, or even at the student station, where there are myriad supplies I can use.

Some teachers will balk and say, "Hey, I spend all day in this room, and I need it to work for me. Don't tell me to get rid of my desk." Of course! If you are not happy, your students will not be happy. You have to do what works for you. As long as you stay cognizant of the message you are sending to your students in regards to the placement of furniture in the room, you will be serving your students better. Furniture and walls really aren't the key to a transformative culture in our classrooms. The key is how we treat students. Consider trusting them to make some of these choices for you.

SHIFT THE WALLS OUTSIDE YOUR CLASSROOM

» Who is "in charge" of the hallways?

» Who decorates the classroom door and surrounding area?

» How can you allow students more choice in decorating this space?

Let's extend student choice in decorating to the spaces *outside* the door of their classroom—the entryway and hallway. Consider the different ways students could share their voice in those public spaces. Need some ideas? What about a March Madness book bracket? Allow students to decide what books to include, get the word out to involve the student body in the voting, and tally the votes. What about an "about me" wall where students create the content? How about a friendly game between classes or grades where students decorate with a theme in mind? Giving responsibilities such as these as opportunities to make their classroom environment more kid-friendly and student-driven lets your students know you trust them to make decisions. Is it okay if the idea flops? Sure! If students are given the time to reflect on how they did, they will most likely be motivated to do a better job with the next decoration. Guide and encourage them to use their ideas and creativity. And sure, you'll be there to help. You can stand behind them if they need to use a chair or step stool; or better yet, let the younger ones decorate at their level—so they can see their creations more clearly each day!

The ideas don't have to be confined to decorations. For example, students in my homeroom have set up a "glasses cleaning station" in the hall on Thursdays. It consists of a step stool, a half-used roll of toilet paper, a spray bottle of glass cleaner, and a garbage can. Students set up in the hall during homeroom, and put away their supplies when the bell rings for the first class. The entire school can benefit from this simple, useful station just outside our classroom. Who benefits from the space outside your classroom? How can you make that space even more welcoming?

SHIFT YOUR VIRTUAL SPACE

» How can I connect with parents outside of the classroom?

» How can I encourage students to continue learning outside the classroom?

» How can I make our class materials accessible to students and parents?

» How can I keep parents from being surprised when they walk in and see what we're doing?

» How can I be more proactive in letting students and parents know what's going on?

Create (or Update) Your Class Website

You may already have a class website. If you don't (yet), that alone will be a big shift for you. Your class website's main job is helping you communicate with students and parents. I've made two changes to my site to help achieve that goal. The first small shift was a name change that coincided with a change in purpose. Originally, my site was named

"Kirr Homework." Now it is "Scholars in Room 239." Naming it is half the battle! What message do you want your website to convey? My first attempt in naming my site was factual, but not very inspiring.

Whether you're setting up a classroom website for the first time or you want to update your site, take a look at other teachers' websites and see how they have theirs set up. Check out the various models here: tinyurl.com/ShiftWebsites. (I modeled my site after the work of Paul Solarz, a fifth-grade teacher in my district.) Ask teachers at your own school to send you the link to their sites. Do a Google search for "classroom website" and see the myriad websites other teachers have created.

If you don't have a site yet, you'll need to decide upon a platform. Paul Solarz and I and many other educators use Weebly, but there are a number of options available, including Wix, WordPress, Blogger, Google Sites, etc. Your goal is to find one that is easy for *you* to use. If you get stuck as you set up your site, you can always conduct an Internet inquiry on "how to create a _____ (Weebly, Wix, WordPress, Blogger, Google Sites, etc.) website" to find step-by-step tutorials.

Once you've selected a platform, give your site a name and add a little information about yourself. This can be a tiny blurb on the side or an entire dedicated page. I created a short video using Explain Everything to go along with a script I had ready. I can edit this each year fairly easily, and then upload it to our class website. This way, during Open House or Meet the Teacher night, I don't need to talk about myself; I can talk about our classroom culture and plans for the year.

I have learned that it is best to be proactive with parents. Your site is an excellent place to share your mission (see below) and even a list of reading material that has influenced your own teaching. While you're at it, go ahead and add the curriculum you'll be covering and the standards you'll tackle.

STATE YOUR MISSION

Another shift that will help you focus on your students is to write and publish a mission statement. What do you truly believe? What are your hopes for your students? Write down your beliefs and post them where you will see them daily. I keep mine on my filing cabinet so I can be reminded of them each day. I've included my mission statement below. If you happen to have the same desires and beliefs, by all means—copy, share, and live it!

My mission as a middle-school teacher is

... to improve the lives of those around me.

... to spread optimism and hope.

... to make the teaching experience fun and relevant for the students as well as for myself.

... to expect more of the student than he expects of himself.

... to challenge the student to go beyond her own perceived limitations.

... to be a great listener and a great role model of high integrity.

... to provide a hunger for students to want to learn more.

... to help the next generation fulfill their potential and become successful human beings.

... to always expect more of myself as a teacher with ongoing training and development.

SMILE!

With your website up and running, you're ready for the next shift: putting student photos on the class site. You will need parent permission to post student photos on your classroom's website. This can be acquired through the school's "Acceptable Use Policy" or through a blanket email or letter sent to parents, asking for their signature. Assure parents that you'll never use their child's last name, and that you will take down anything of which they do not approve.

If you want your website to be accessed often by parents, shift the photographer duties over to the students. I usually do this after our first month of school. Explain the guidelines for what the duty involves and then send around a clipboard, asking students to write their names if they'd like to be a photographer. I publish a six-to-nine minute Animoto video every two weeks, using photos my students have taken on a classroom iPad. Our guidelines are simple:

- Remember who the audience for the pictures/video is (the parents and possibly administration).

- Take five to six photos per day per class (for a total of fifteen to eighteen images per day per video).

That's it. Our class photographers also end up learning the skill of editing their images. Some students take 100 photos, then have to whittle it down to six. Occasionally, I'll see photos turn up in a PicCollage, which they then put on the camera roll, so they can cleverly use more than six photos in this fashion.

Tip: Keep all the photos in one location so students can create a movie for the end of the year! (A classroom computer or a shared folder on Google Drive works well.) Check out our parent updates and student photos here: tinyurl.com/ShiftParentUpdates.

SHARE GOOD VIBES

Like so many aspects of our lives, parent communication has become more "virtual" in recent years. Yes, a website is a great resource for parents, but email is also a very important tool. I use both. I email the parents the link to the parent update on the website every two weeks.

My reward is when the parents thank me or when students say their parents watch our slideshows.

A personal way to use communication to build community is to let individual parents know about the positive impact their child is having in the classroom. Call home or send a personal note via email. Make a deliberate effort to communicate to individual parents about their children. Yes, this takes time. Yes, you need to be intentional when you decide to implement this. I've got my student list and a chart of when I've sent emails home. After two years of practice, I can now contact each parent at least twice during the year. If I had one class, I'd try to make it more frequent, and if I had 150 students, I'd probably be satisfied with one personal contact. Often, the subject line of my emails is "Saturday Sunshine," as I send them on Saturday mornings. At other times, it's "Fabulous Friday" or "Terrific Tuesday"—you get the idea. Many parents are used to only receiving messages from teachers when there is an issue or something is troubling regarding their child, so make sure the subject line says something positive. Save parents the undue angst by putting positive words in the subject line. "Good News" works just fine! Sometimes I write a draft and use an app called Boomerang to send the email later in the week—on Saturday morning.

How do you know what to say or whom to email? Easy! Make a mental note of who has demonstrated leadership, or the child who is always positive, or the student who contributed unexpectedly, etc. Parents will appreciate the fact that you noticed their child and took the extra step to contact them. The bonus is that students love the letters home too. They come to school the next day with a huge smile or a "thank you" or bragging to the other students because I wrote to their parents. One parent told me that her daughter posted a printed copy of the email on her bedroom wall! I truly feel that these surprise notes or phone calls home make a difference in how students act in class. The messages cultivate trust, and that goes a looooong way in developing the positive culture of your classroom. If you need more guidance, follow Rik Rowe (@RoweRikW) or #GoodCallsHome on Twitter to see how other teachers handle these, as well as the rewards they reap. Want to get techie with it by frontloading the work of names and emails and saving tons of time when you're sending them? Check out Michael Matera's (@mrmatera) truly magical Mail Merge idea and directions: tinyurl.com/ShiftMailMerge.

Make Good Vibes a Class Effort

Let's then shift the power of these good notes home to your students. Invite your students to observe the positive behaviors of others in the classroom. Consider setting up a jar in your classroom with paper next to it. This will be for positive peer feedback. Here's what the slips in room 239 look like:

Please share this message with _____
(Consider mature behavior, risk-taking for the benefit of all, kindness...)

Contributor's name: _____
Block (circle one):   4/5   6/8   9/10

Students can now write their own message. Make it simpler for younger children using symbols they can circle. When you email parents, your subject line can read "Positive Peer Feedback." The message template can look like this:

You have now put more power in your students' hands. Students, parents, and peers all win.

Please share this message with _____:

(Insert good vibes here.)

We thought you should know!
~_____'s (teacher) class

This message was sent as a result of our "positive peer feedback jar,"
which students can contribute to any day of the week to send recognition
to a classmate for a job well done.

INVITE PARENTS IN

One way to make your classroom less of an unknown and more *real* to parents is to invite them in. Invite. Them. In. I started inviting parents into our room after we had a group of them come to our Cardboard Challenge (do a search for "Caine's Arcade" and join in the fun and learning). One parent told me she comes to school every time she's invited because she feels that her opportunities for classroom participation are so limited. She said that once her children hit sixth grade, she "never gets into the classroom." In other words, she *wanted* to be more involved. Her statement stayed with me. And when our new superintendent challenged our school on Opening Day with a message titled "If you weren't afraid, what would you do?" I knew it was time to invite parents into the classroom.

Although it was my twentieth year of teaching, I was still a bit nervous around parents of my students. I know the responsibility I have, and I am aware that their children are in front of me every day. I wanted parents to know I take this honor and responsibility seriously. So I jumped in, answering the call of both my superintendent and a parent. I used a tool called "Sign Up Genius," and asked parents to join us for book talks or read-alouds. See our success story at tinyurl.com/ShiftParentsIn. This has been one of the best parts of our year, and parents and students alike enjoy the visits.

Parents (and grandparents) *love* to come into our classes. When you invite them often, they'll see that you really do mean it, and start to feel more comfortable coming. If they begin coming in regularly, they'll make connections with students and you'll see some students in a new light. "Grammie" came into our classes weekly for two years in a row—during Genius Hour. I could ask her to check in with students regarding their goals for the next two weeks or their plans for the day. Sometimes I asked her to work with one particular child. Other times the kids came right up to her and shared what they were doing. Grammie (yes, that's what we called her—she was one of my student's grandmothers) told me that her life was enriched each week because of these visits. She was a "regular," and when she couldn't make it, the kids were bummed. She laughed and cried with us, loved the children, and they knew it. Soon she was a school sensation, and children were giving her hugs when they spotted her in the hallways! She even came the next year when her grandson had moved on to eighth grade, and this year she's coming in again for our independent inquiry projects—and I'm so grateful! Invite parents and grandparents in, and see how your classroom culture shifts. (To see more on how she impacted us, read the blog post note of thanks here: tinyurl.com/ShiftGrammie.)

SHIFT CLASSROOM CULTURE

» How can I let students know they matter to me?

» How can I learn who these students are so that I can better teach them individually?

» How can I encourage risk-taking so students put forth effort and become empowered?

» How can I encourage each child to share and then collaborate with one another?

#1st5days

Culture is the foundation of the classroom community. It is not just the physical room that sends a message to students; the evidence of what you value—shown on the walls and on your class website—speaks volumes. You establish your classroom culture in the first five days of class, so to the list of questions above, you may want to add this one:

» What message do I send to students the first five days of class?

If you're looking for ideas to build a strong, positive culture from the first day of school, check out the Twitter hashtag, #1st5days, which was started by Alan November (novemberlearning.com). It gets a lot of action in August in the United States! Additionally, I have created a "LiveBinder" online and filled it with activities you can use to make your first five days with students valuable. You can access it at tinyurl.com/Shift1st5days. The activities you'll find in both the binder and at #1st5days will inspire you to ditch the "old view" that you must go over the rules and your syllabus with students those days. Instead, use that precious time to get to know your students while helping them learn more about one another.

 Invite parents and grandparents in, and see how your classroom culture shifts.

One way to set the tone of your class is by giving them challenges that promote collaboration. Activities in the online binder include the Marshmallow Challenge, where students are encouraged to build the tallest freestanding marshmallow structure within a certain amount of time with a certain amount of supplies. Food allergies? Try the other team building games available that promote critical thinking. Want it a bit quieter? Throw out a controversial question and start practicing fishbowl discussions with students. Or perhaps you'd like to give a questionnaire or survey to find out about students' interests, strengths, and struggles. One way to get students up and moving is to craft survey questions into a "human bingo" type of game—students can search for others in the group who can "say a sentence in sign language" or "play an instrument." This way students are up and moving, and you can interact with them in a more relaxed way.

What's in a Name?

Find a way to learn *every student's name* the very first day (or very first week if you have many different classes). Setting up the first days in this manner sends a strong message to students: They matter. They will be asked to work with one another throughout the year for the greater good of the class as a whole. Learning the names of students shows that you are interested in them and that you are approachable. It builds trust, shows you care, and encourages other students to interact with one another more easily.

Respect, Not Rules

If you begin your school year by sending the message that your students matter—that you really care about and are interested in them—you may find that you don't need to create a classroom set of rules. Students will learn through daily practice and reflection that you value respect above all—for people, for supplies, and for ideas that will be shared throughout the year.

Think of how many teachers students see, and how many rules are meant to be followed for each one. Even at the elementary level, there are rules for their main class, and rules for music class, art class, and any other "specials." How do they learn how to keep it all straight? That's a lot to ask of a child—of any age. Before you consider giving rules, consider allowing them to learn about one another. The more they learn about one another, the more likely they are to be considerate of their peers and naturally follow society's rules. I especially think this is important at the middle and high school level. Put yourself in their shoes. Would you like to attend eight or so lectures regarding rules and the syllabus on the first day of school, or would you rather be engaged right away in meaningful learning about your peers? Keep these questions in mind as you plan out your days. You know those adolescents aren't wondering what the rules are—they're wondering what type of year they're going to experience (along with who is in their classes). They're wondering what type of teacher you are as well. Are you more concerned about them or about rules?

Celebrate Each Day

As the year progresses, be wary of countdowns. I am embarrassed that I used to join in countdowns to our winter, spring, and summer breaks. Heck, I used to *lead* them! Countdowns seem like they are helping classroom culture, but what's the message you're sending if you join in? Do you want students to think you don't want to be in school, either? I'm not saying I'm a saint or that I don't need breaks from school, just like the kids. I prefer, however, to celebrate each day I have with students. I encourage you to find another way to celebrate with your class. (See more thoughts in the comments here: tinyurl.com/ShiftCountdowns.)

FURTHER READING

» Classroom Cribs: classroomcribs.com/hi

» Deskless Tribe: desklesstribe.com

» Flexible Seating Student-Centered Classroom: edutopia.org/blog/flexible-seating-student-centered-classroom-kayla-delzer

» *Kids Deserve It!*: kidsdeserveit.com/about-us

» Michael Matera, *Explore Like a Pirate: Engage, Enrich, and Elevate Your Learners with Gamification and Game-Inspired Course Design* (Dave Burgess Consulting: 2015)

» The Physical Environment of Classrooms: edutopia.org/blog/the-physical-environment-of-classrooms-mark-phillips

REFLECTION AND CALL TO ACTION

» What does your classroom look like to the students? Sit in different places around the room and imagine being in that spot for a while. Heck—sit in other classrooms too. What do you notice about the physical look of the place? What would distract you? Lure you? Welcome you?

» How could you change your classroom environment to be more welcoming?

» What do you call your room? If you believe your room is not really *your* room, how can you make the name of your room more appealing to your students?

» How could you promote collaboration among students during the first five days? Research the #1st5days hashtag or LiveBinder (tinyurl.com/Shift1st5days) and jot down five ideas you'd like to try.

» How will you let students know you value their opinion during the first five days—and throughout the rest of the school year?

_____

_____

_____

_____

_____

5 | Classwork

Your words matter more than you know.

—*A Snicker of Magic* by Natalie Lloyd

"*C*an we have a fishbowl today?"

"This time can we put an actual fish in the fishbowl discussion?"

"Why won't it work today? What are we talking about?"

This is when I have to stop and remind students that in order to have a quality fishbowl discussion, the question has to come from them, and it has to be somewhat controversial. Their brains start churning, and you can almost see them generating questions in their minds to ask so they can have that fishbowl discussion they so very much want to participate in.

Classwork = any work you do *in* class. This includes anything you're expected to do (including curriculum you must cover), and the choices you are allowed. How can we make shifts to what we're expected to teach? That question and more plague me every day.

» How can I engage my students more with this scripted curriculum I am expected to teach?

» Should I choose partners for the kids or let them choose for themselves?

» How can I make sure all students are contributing to group work?

» How can I involve more students in our whole-class discussions?

» How can I engage those students who "only put forth the effort if they're interested"?

» How can the class know the thoughts of those who don't speak in class?

» How can we *all* share ideas in order to learn from one another?

» How can students learn to use more precise language when talking with one another?

» How can I provide time for students to do most of the talking in class?

» How can we encourage everyone to contribute so I am not the "sage on the stage," and I am instead the "guide on the side"?

Let's now focus on how you can shift class lessons more towards the students and give the students more ownership over classwork.

SHIFT YOUR LESSONS

You've been given the lessons. They're prepackaged, and anyone who can read can follow them. You begin, and a lesson or two in, students are already checking out. They're with you, but only enough to do the bare minimum. Unless you've memorized the lesson and the script, it may seem as if you're giving the bare minimum as well. Children know when you know your lessons and are passionate about them; they also know when you're not invested in them, or are uncomfortable or unfamiliar with lessons.

Try Different Modalities

If the plans call for students to write the answers every time, try having them show the answer somehow on their hands instead (numbers and sign language letters work well for this). Perhaps use small white boards to share. Try having them move to one part of the room or another for certain multiple choice or opinion questions. Ask them to shout out their answers. Of course, this can get loud, and they might actually enjoy it. Have them write their answers on each other's backs (using clipboards or notebooks), then read their answers to each other first before sharing with the class.

Go Off Script

If you find that part of the curriculum doesn't work for your students, it's time to shift again. Yes! It's okay to veer off the plan. No administrator who cares about student achievement would want you to continue with any plan that isn't working. This goes for scripted lessons as well as lessons you've designed. If you can be sure your students understand the material, let them know that you're skipping some sections, and do a quick review. Then move on.

Some teachers fear trying this shift, but think of it this way: You're doing what's best for your specific students. What curriculum is failproof? What curriculum fits *every* child? Education is your expertise. You are paid to teach, not just read pre-set lesson plans. Step up to that role by getting to know your students and adjusting the curriculum to fit their needs.

Gamify Your Lessons

Do you need more engagement in the lessons? Consider gamifying the lesson or unit. Gamification is simply applying game elements to other situations. Michael Matera, in *Explore Like a Pirate*, suggests looking for ways to gamify what you are already doing. Can you make the discussion worth virtual points when students use text support?

Can you divvy up the class into three groups and have them compete for coming up with the best review questions? Simple games (that could lead up to elaborate exploration and year-long game play) could bring scripted lessons to life and help make your students perk up and learn more as a result of their engagement with the curriculum.

Ask for Student Input

If you're trying curriculum you're not familiar with, create a way for students to give feedback on how it's going. Consider a quick Google form or quarter sheet of paper with two questions:

1. What went well today?

2. What suggestions do you have for improvement?

Let students know you will be getting their feedback to the writers of the curriculum. Go a step further and look at the feedback yourself to decide how you can improve your plans the very next day. Of course, you can do this *any* time—even with the lessons *you* designed. You can bet your students will have suggestions for improvement that you hadn't ever imagined.

Keep the End in Mind

The last shift in any scripted curriculum is to keep the goal of the lesson in mind and add to (or remove from) the curriculum anything that will help students get closer to the goal. Can you take a day in between lessons to ask students to find supplemental resources? Better yet, can you ask students to teach a lesson in their own way? You will have to plan ahead with students, but it's worth doing so to help students take charge of their own learning.

SHIFT PARTNER AND SMALL GROUP WORK

Sometimes a lesson (scripted or not) calls for partners or small groups. Use your discretion and decide when each is appropriate. If your students are sluggish one day, make the small groups partner work instead. If your students have a lot of energy, combine those partners into small groups of four. (It's also a great time for your students to practice moving your tables or desks!)

Who Chooses the Groups—and How?

When it comes time to choose partners or groups, do you make those decisions, or do the students? There are many random-name generators online these days. Look up "random name generator," and they'll be easy to spot—and use. I use an app called "Pick Me" with student photos that show up when you press the button marked "spin," or group the students in any size number group. Of course, you can randomly draw Popsicle sticks (with students' names on them) from a cup. (Add a toilet paper roll in the middle of the cup for calling on students, and you only need one cup per class. All of the sticks can start in the middle of the toilet paper roll. When you use one, place it back in the cup outside the roll. Or vice-versa.) You can use clothespins with students' names instead—putting them on cups or on a paper hanging from the bulletin board. Assign students numbers, and call out math problems to pair students or put them in groups. There are many ways to select pairs or groups of students. When my students are put with people randomly, I give them a question to help break the ice and learn something about the other person or people in the group.

> Getting to know you questions (and explanations)
> are located here: **tinyurl.com/ShiftGetToKnowYou.**

Or maybe, you want to give the ultimate choice to your class. This is one shift that is easy to implement and puts responsibility on students. Post this statement and the following choices on the board at the start of class and have students move their name magnets by the option they prefer:

We're having small groups today.
I am responsible enough to choose my own group.
I would like the teacher to choose my group.
Either way is fine with me.

When it comes time to choose groups, the teacher chooses for the last two groups, and the first group chooses its own. This is a common question in my "question of the day" toolbox.

SHIFT DISCUSSIONS

One of the beautiful benefits of partner and group work is that there is no hand raising. Children learn how to have true discussions—by listening, responding, and taking turns. As Kelly Gallagher explains in his book, *In the Best Interest of Students*, speaking and listening skills "are foundational to becoming literate human beings." These skills help us learn from one another, and learning from others helps us become more empathetic and understanding. Children don't come into this world knowing how to communicate effectively. It's a skill we need to practice, practice, practice, and not solely in language arts classes. Consider the possibilities when students are sharing evidence gleaned from science labs, evidence from each side of a specific war in history class, or decision-making in health class. Choosing precise words to communicate effectively takes time to practice, and the classroom should serve as a safe environment in which to fail and try again. Beyond the classroom, learning to communicate effectively will help your students as they enter the marketplace since communication skills are among the highest priorities for employers.

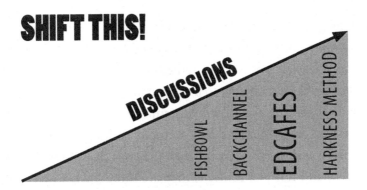

Whole-Class Discussions

Class discussions are where magic happens in a classroom—*if* they're done well. The trick is for the teacher to not be the one talking, and for there to be no hand raising. This student-led, free flow of conversation is a far cry from "the way we've always done it," but the more shifts you make toward student-run discussions, the more your students will glean from each discussion.

If you aren't already having class discussions, introduce the idea and ask your students, "Why should we discuss things in class?" "Why should we have discussions?" or "What's the value in discussions?" Jot down every child's idea, whether you think it's good or not so good, where all can see them. Another way to generate answers is to have students come up to the board and write them down themselves. In this discussion, you, as teacher, are still a leader. Go over each of these ideas separately, then ask students to help you pare them down to a solid three to five reasons that emphasize the value of discussions. Take a photo of the final selections or write them down so that students can refer to them time and time again throughout the year.

Now that you've got reasons why, do the same with the "how to." Ask students, "What can we do that will help us have valuable discussions?" Accumulate all the ideas, then, with the students deciding, help them create a list of five to ten ideas. Before you document their ideas, ask students to take one more step and prioritize them. Which should come first? Prioritizing may help weed out some suggestions that are similar, or it may help students combine two into one to make these more feasible and easy to remember. Here are some ways my students have shared in order to have valuable discussions: one person at a time, support one another by listening and bouncing off of their ideas, respect other opinions, stay on topic, and use evidence or support when you share an opinion. How precious that these ideas came from them and not me! It means they are more likely to be invested with the ideas and have valuable discussions with one another.

When it's time to try a whole-class discussion, pose a question that will generate some opinions on both sides, such as "Should junk food be sold in the cafeteria?" Ask the question, reminding students of their suggestions as to how to have a good discussion. It helps students stay on topic and focused on the discussion if you ask them to first write down their answers along with the reasons why they believe that answer is correct. Next, have students split off to opposite sides of the room, depending on their views. Separating out into two sides, or even four corners (when there are four possible answers), is a good way to structure your first few classroom discussions. The children who answered "yes" can go to one side, and those who answered "no" to the other. Let students know that throughout the discussion, they can move sides if they change their mind. This prevents students from sitting in the middle and not participating. (Plus, we know it's good for the kids to get out of their seats!) Ask for volunteers on each side of the room to share their thoughts.

When the discussion begins to dwindle or after a set time you've chosen, ask students to help list what went well during the discussion and what they need to change. This could include respect, volume, content, and even behaviors of the students not sharing ideas.

After creating this list, pose another question: In what circumstances would people have discussions outside of school? (Possible answers: the kitchen table, a board room at a company, after watching a movie together, when friends are over, at a birthday party, etc.) What's the difference between their classroom discussion and "real-life" discussions? Do most people walk to a part of the room to share their views? Do most people raise their hands to take a turn? Help students find out that there are more things they can change to help them have better discussions. Possible ideas include the following:

» Moving the seating so students are facing one another.

» Having fewer people.

» No side conversations.

Go back and try a new discussion and encourage the kids to figure out how to not raise hands and still take turns. Options students might come up with that could help them take turns are making eye contact, saying the next student's name, nodding, or asking a helpful question such as, "Does anyone think differently?" If students ask you a question, ask it back to the class to see what they think. Try your best to not answer their questions; let them figure out their own answers instead. Reflect after this discussion again, asking what students did well and what they could change. Many times, items under "what we need to change" are the same. This is your cue to introduce fishbowl discussions.

If students ask you a question, ask it back to the class to see what they think. Try your best to not answer their questions; let them figure out their own answers instead.

Fishbowl Discussions

No hands raised, students taking turns, using eye contact and gestures—is this a dream class? In some ways, yes, but it can happen in many classrooms—I've see it work! When your students have practiced discussions a few times, your next step could be to implement fishbowl discussions. I've learned most of what I know about the dynamics of fishbowl discussions from Paul Bogush's video explanation (tinyurl.com/ShiftFishbowl); my students have taught me the rest! The reasons we should implement fishbowl discussions are clear: We want students to participate in their learning, so that they can learn even more. Student voices should be the most heard in the student-centered classroom. The teacher does not participate, and students sitting around the center circle are more focused on what is said in the inner circle than in a typical classroom discussion. Fishbowl discussions are typically two-sided, and students need to listen carefully to what is being said so they can then refute or enhance their peers' views with relevant evidence. When it goes well, even if students do not come to a consensus, this activity cultivates a culture of trust and respect for one another.

The gist: Up to six students sit in a circle in the middle of the room. I start with four and let students suggest adding another chair or two as we become more familiar with the way fishbowl conversations run. The other students sit outside of this circle, in a bigger circle. The inner circle is where the discussion takes place. Students on the outside of the circle are observers (and notetakers at the higher grades). They have the ability to join in the discussion after it gets going. Once students in the middle have had their say in the discussion, or have asked another question to keep the group talking, a student from the outer circle can tap on that student's shoulder and come in to the discussion to add his or her thoughts and ideas.

Paul lays out a few rules in his video:

- Only one person speaks at a time.

- Participants must use clues such as body language and eye contact to determine when to speak. If two people speak, one must hold back.

- Questions can only be asked by people in the inner circle.

- Respond to comments by adding additional evidence or asking questions.

- If you have the opportunity to say your ideas, make sure you support them with evidence.

- To leave or enter, the person must tag another individual.

- If you're leaving the bowl, you have to pick someone who hasn't entered in a long time.

- You have to say something meaningful before you leave the fishbowl.

- Each person must connect their thought with a previous one and end with a question for the group.

- The conversation does not just exist so you can hear yourself talk; it exists so the group can explore an idea or question.

- The words may not be the most important ones spoken, but will reflect on other statements.

- People on the outside must write down statements that make you go, *Hmm, ahhh,* or *huh?*

Discuss these with students prior to your first fishbowl discussion. To involve them more and get their investment in this type of discussion, ask for their input on the rules. What would they like to definitely keep? Are there any rules they think need tweaking? Take the time to prepare students for these discussions, or your first one will flop for sure. (It might anyway, but I've found the preparation is worth it—and it helps your students want to try it right away and do it well!) Along with the rules, ask students how they'd like to see the room arranged for this. Have a seating arrangement ready to project, just in case students can't figure it out. Practice moving the chairs and desks or tables, and time it! You'll see those natural leaders take charge and help students figure out how it should all go.

Before you actually have a fishbowl discussion, make sure you have a topic in mind. Not every question works well for this type of discussion. (And some you think will work well can flop, based on the participants and their opinions.) For example, seventh graders love to talk about gum in school. If I posed the question, "Should we allow gum in school?" 95 percent or more of my current students would say, "YES!" This discussion wouldn't last one minute unless there was a student in the class who knows what the custodians go through. Likewise, a question such as "Should we have recess?" or "Should we have show-and-tell?" might not work at the younger levels.

However, questions such as "Should we have nap time?" or "Should students be required to wear school uniforms?" are a bit more controversial and make for better discussions. The most effective questions allow for multiple opinions. It's rewarding to teachers when students are empathetic and can look at the question through a different perspective. The older your students, the more mature and impactful the discussions can be. Remember, however, that effective discussions can happen at any age, and from most any subject matter.

After your first class fishbowl discussion, reflect with students as to what they did well and how they could improve. One suggestion for improvement might be making the group smaller. It is possible to have the same question in two groups when you have enough students. Another suggestion to help the group focus is to give students in the outer circle responsibilities. When you provide time for reflection, students will often come up with ideas to make the discussions go smoother that you might not have considered otherwise. Before you conduct your next fishbowl discussion, bring up their reflections and review their ideas for how to improve.

If your class has trouble finding participants for the middle of the fishbowl, it could be because students don't feel comfortable answering the question or think it is "too boring." In either case, you can try a hat trick—put six (or however many you want in the middle circle) index cards of one color in a hat, and twenty-four (or however many other students you have) of another color in the hat, then have students choose randomly. The students who chose the six of one color will be the first participants for that particular discussion.

At higher grade levels, you can promote participation from the students in the outer circle by asking them to take notes. If that request is too vague for them, ask them to take notes on a certain seat (for any student in that seat) in the middle circle. What words or ideas did that person share or notice that are strong points and/or could be revisited? Another variation is to have groups of three. One student from each group is the "fish" (in the bowl), and the other two can "feed the fish." They can write down ideas and slip the paper/index card/sticky note to the "fish" in the middle. Reflection after each discussion—about participation as well as other aspects of the discussion—is integral to helping the students get better each time.

Backchannel Discussions

The next step is to offer some sort of backchannel to students in the outer circle. A backchannel is a way for students to join in on the conversation without uttering a sound. If your students are old enough and have Twitter accounts, they can use a pre-determined hashtag (ex: #ClassPer3) to share their thoughts. They can then just follow that hashtag and add to it as they have thoughts. This is an excellent way to take notes as well. This also benefits you as the teacher, as you've got their ideas to go back to and share or discuss at a later date. You can see who is paying close attention, who doesn't understand what's being discussed, and who is not participating.

If your students do not have Twitter accounts, try a tool called "TodaysMeet" that allows teachers to create a "room" and set the time span students will have to join this "room." Students put in their first names, and can "discuss" the inside circle conversation online. This is not open to the general public—students must have a link in order to access the virtual room. The teacher can monitor student comprehension and can boot anyone off a discussion if he or she is not being respectful. Other backchannel tools include Socrative, Backchannel Chat, and Padlet (like a sticky note board). You can even use a Google Doc shared with all students to keep track of student participation.

If you still have a few students who don't join in the discussion, consider asking them to be the "scribes." This ensures they are listening. You can also share these notes with students afterwards to see how the conversation shifted over time. The next step could be to put the discussion notes online for all students to see and share with their parents! Research "backchannel classroom discussions" online to find more that can work for you and your students.

How could younger children have a backchannel? Consider "take two" or "turn and talk." Stop the discussion in the middle, and have the participants on the outside take a minute or two and discuss what they're observing or thinking. When you ask them to share out ideas, write them down. Now the participants in the middle have more food for thought.

EdCafes

EdCafes are another shift that will empower your students to drive more of the learning. Here's the gist: Students read or listen to something assigned to them. It could be short stories, math word problems, scientific studies, current news, or recent research. They then generate questions about what they wonder or what confuses them. As a whole class, these questions are projected or written on the board, and then four questions (more or less depending on how many groups you can have) are chosen for discussion points. Designate a space for each discussion. Students then move to that space to discuss the question in which they're most interested.

Figuring out which four questions could be difficult when you first try this idea. Students will need guidance in order to determine what makes a good discussion question. I like to eliminate obvious ones first. Any that have a "yes" or "no" answer are quickly out of the running unless the class is split with their answers. Likewise, any that most of the class agrees upon should be out. Next, come right out and ask, "Which one of these could you probably talk a long time about? Which one do you think, if you searched hard enough, you'd find some evidence for in a text or video?" In ELA, my favorite question from a text is "How old is the main character?" This works particularly well with *The Night I Won the Right to the Streets of Memphis* by Richard Wright. Students can use text evidence and what they know about responsibility, family, the time period, and even Memphis to support their answers.

I love EdCafes because it gives even more ownership to the students. They get to talk, in small groups, about values, math, the government, science, or just for fun. It is the most authentic type of discussion I think you can have with a class size of twenty or more students. It is more like a discussion at the dinner table than the other methods I've shared, and it's exciting to see the students so involved. After each group discusses, have them share out what they decide are important points to consider. Also ask if anyone changed their mind as a result of ideas shared in the conversation.

> For more on EdCafes, check out this video from
> Katrina Kennett: **tinyurl.com/ShiftEdCafe.**

Harkness Method

What's next? Ask students to put the furniture back in place, of course! Actually, you could go a giant step further. You could try what's called the "Harkness Method" every day. Your whole world can flip upside down (in a good way!) if your school decides to implement this. I was fortunate to speak at and visit Second Baptist School in Houston, Texas, where I was able to sit in one classroom where students were discussing Texas history prior to the Civil War. Students had notes on their homework from the night before and were using them to guide their discussion. They brought the questions to the large conference table, and they took turns figuring out their wonders, confusions, and misunderstandings. The students did most of the talking, and the teacher was there to guide their discussion when it got off track or when they couldn't answer one another. This method works well with small classes or groups of twelve to fourteen students.

STUDENTS LEAD

Once you discover your students' passions, let them take the lead. Perhaps they can teach the class something they love. Imagine if what they loved meshed with what you needed other students to know! Perhaps their passions can be used to introduce various discussion methods. Consider letting a student choose an article or a video to discuss. Maybe one student really loves sedimentary rocks and has a question that's been on his mind. Use that as the catalyst to begin a discussion! Maybe one student can share design strategies using their passion for Legos. Another student has a great way to remember multiplication facts for the number nine. Imagine how much more engaging your content will be when you trust students to lead. These opportunities are often spur of the moment, but feel free to plan them ahead of time! Give children the practice in class so they can learn from one another.

FURTHER READING

» A Look At The Harkness Method Of Teaching (schoolnetuganda.com/study-tips/ a-look-at-the-harkness-method-of-teaching/)

» Alan November, *Who Owns the Learning? Preparing Students for Success in the Digital Age* (Solution Tree Press: 2012)

» Angela Maiers and Amy Sandvold, *The Passion-Driven Classroom: A Framework for Teaching & Learning* (Larchmont: 2011)

» Beth Holland, "The Backchannel: Giving Every Student a Voice in the Blended Mobile Classroom" (edutopia.org/blog/ backchannel-student-voice-blended-classroom-beth-holland)

» Kelly Gallagher, *In the Best Interest of Students: Staying True to What works in the ELA Classroom* (Stenhouse: 2015)

REFLECTION AND CALL TO ACTION

» Consider recording a lesson (or a day). Listen to the recording and compare how much of the day you speak versus how much of the day the students speak. What do you think of that ratio? If it is not acceptable to you, what could you incorporate tomorrow to help your students speak more in class?

» What discussions about content could students in your class have?

» What type of choice could you provide students when it comes to discussions?

» How will you get more students involved in your next class discussion? Consider low-risk speaking activities. How can you include student interest to engage those students who do not participate?

» How will you make your class discussions more authentic—more like "real life"? School is real life! How can you step away from the "teacher questions and student responds" type of teaching?

» Which method do you think best fits your next unit?

_____

_____

_____

6 Homework

I wonder about the deep, wide abyss between
good intentions and concrete action...

—*The Running Dream* by Wendelin Van Draanen

S tudent: *"What if I didn't read last night?"*

Me: *"Then you didn't do your homework."*

Student: *"But you're not checking, right? Or are
you? How would you know if I didn't tell you?"*

Me: *"Reading skills accumulate over time. We'll both know
when it's time to assess your comprehension skills. You'll also
be bummed out when you haven't developed the stamina of
reading each night and suddenly it's a requirement to read
something your teacher wants you to read."*

On our board, under a sign that reads "Independent Practice"
instead of "Homework," a student in my homeroom writes, "Read for
20 minutes." This is the only homework in our seventh grade ELA class
on most days. It may not be perfect, as many students do not read each
night, but I believe that because it's there on a daily basis, week after
week, month after month, it will get into their heads that I believe daily
reading outside of school is very important. Since not every child will

do this work, I also give time during class for them to read their independent choice books.

Before I changed my homework procedures, I asked myself and then researched these *questions*:

» How much is too much homework?

» How much homework are other teachers giving their students?

» What should children be doing after school to help retain what they learned during school?

» How can we foster getting children outside and sociable after school (instead of on their devices or playing video games)?

This chapter will focus on how you can slowly let go of monopolizing students' time after school. My dream is that students will want to do work outside of the school hours that would support my curriculum, if I can instill in them a love of learning in school.

SHIFT HOMEWORK QUANTITY

It's the Goldilocks principle all over again: how much homework is "just right" for your students? In elementary school, you may be the only one who dictates the amount of homework for your students. Conversations with other teachers in your grade may help you determine what works best regarding the amount of homework. In middle and high school, other teachers and content-area specialists (all of which most likely believe that their subject level is the most important) will have their own homework procedures. Don't operate in a silo. Find out how much time your fellow teachers expect their students to spend outside of school on their subject. Should it matter? Which class (if any) should get first priority?

Once you know how much homework other teachers in your current grade are assigning, start conversations with your students and their parents. How can any teachers decide how much homework is right for every child in their class? How can you find out what the "right" amount is? Trial and error. Ask your students. Ask the parents of your students. Seek advice, conduct surveys, and try to plan this with a teaching partner. You do not have to go this route alone.

Without even looking at what the research says (elementary teachers, please read Alfie Kohn's research, as he finds there is no correlation between homework and improved academic achievement in younger ages), we know that children are becoming more sedentary. You might see this outside your own home. Where are the kids? What happened to playing ball in the street, or heading out to bike around the neighborhood? Video games and computers that happen to fit in our pockets seem to have taken over much of our time. Perhaps it is not the *amount* of homework you need to concern yourself with, but the *type* of homework.

SHIFT HOMEWORK TYPE

Are you still giving worksheets for homework? Consider this question: What if your students fill in the worksheet all wrong? They are suddenly making a habit of learning the wrong thing—tossing what you've supposedly taught them during the school day out the window. They then come to school, turn in their work, and (if you're on the ball and can get them feedback right away) suddenly motivation to learn is gone, because they've failed at the work they thought they knew. Way to derail the next thirty-minute lesson.

What other options are there? What are some choices that will help foster the love of your curriculum and not be problematic? The next series of shifts explains a few different ways you can keep students learning even when they're not at school.

Choice Boards

Do you ever get bored grading the same thing over and over (and over) again? If *you* would like some variety in what gets turned in, chances are students would like some variety as well. Choice fuels engagement, so why not try choice boards?

A variety of choice boards are available online, and of course you can create some with your own flair or theme. Choice boards, simply put, include various ways for students to show what they know about the material. The most common would be a tic-tac-toe board. Students can complete one row of activities across, down, or diagonal. Parameters for choice boards will be the toughest thing you have to decide. How many choices should students need to complete? In what time frame?

Examples of choice boards include simple lists, connect the dots (you decide how many or what type of shape for the result), and tic-tac-toe. One high school math teacher in Arlington, Massachusetts, Rik Rowe, calls his math choices "tic-tac-Rowe." In some tic-tac-toe boards, teachers list multiple items, allowing for even more choice. Use Google Images to search for "choice boards for _____," and see the various work teachers share. Second graders are learning new vocabulary? One choice could be to find how many times "(insert word here)" occurs on two pages of a book at home. Students could draw the book cover and write the number. Consider the multiple intelligences when you're creating choices—some students will thrive at certain skills, and you'll be able to see what they truly know regarding that piece of curriculum. They will also feel more at ease, seeing that they can draw or act or type instead of something that may be more difficult or embarrassing for them.

One of the rewarding aspects of choice boards for teachers is that we get to see our students' other skills shine. Suppose one of the choices is to create a short video explaining a vocabulary word or concept. Students who are skilled at video editing will take this one on and stun you with their editing (and maybe even musical) skills. Receiving assignments such as these in your inbox will not only make you smile, but you can share them with other students, while keeping that student in mind when someone else could use their talent. Feel free to let these activities be a springboard for your "expert wall of fame," an idea from Angela Maiers, that shows who is talented at what, so other students can go to their peers for guidance. Including various choices in homework can lead to finding out each student's particular talents, and creating a community in your classroom where students can go to other students (instead of you) for help during the rest of your school year and beyond. If you teach in the upper grades, be sure to share your students' talents with their other teachers as well! Consider the implications: Showcasing talents empowers the students who don't typically play the "game of school" very well. They can now feel more accepted and valued because you've given them a choice in how to share what they know.

Showcasing talents empowers the students who don't typically play the "game of school" very well.

Flipped Instruction

Worksheets and choice boards aside, what if you didn't collect anything from students once they did their homework? Flipping the classroom can help you make this work. A flipped classroom, at its most basic level, is when teachers put lectures on video for students to watch at home, and then ask students to do the practice work in class. Jason Bretzmann is my go-to guy when it comes to flipping the learning. In *Flipping 2.0*, he states that the true student-centered model is "characterized by focusing on higher-level thinking as a goal, creating a more student-centered classroom, and determining the best use of face-to-face time with students."

The simplest version of a flipped lesson entails recording yourself giving a lesson or lecture and asking students to view it at home. Video length should correlate with students' ages. For example, do not give a twelve-year-old a video that is longer than twelve minutes. (Twelve minutes may be too long for any student, depending on how engaging it is.) Naysayers will declare it can't be done, because not every child has access to technology at home. That's an easy fix—give students time before, or even during, class to watch the short lesson. If this is something you're willing to try, you can find many example lessons online. Once you see the value of flipping one way, you'll get the itch to read the ideas in Jason's book and focus more on the learning—not necessarily the videos.

Challenges

Flipping the classroom still keeps the kids in the house using the computer. It's time to get the kids outside by suggesting some challenges. After all, the world is our school, isn't it?

YouTube is one way our students research. Why not use that to our advantage? The Coke and Mentos experiment will never die. In fact, for years people around the world have been trying many different ways to make a bigger and more fancy scene with these two ingredients. What if you gave each student (or group) four common items and asked them to create something in a given amount of time? What if you kept it wide open and asked students to create something out of cardboard? How about a marshmallow building challenge? Shadow sculpture that represents an aspect of your curriculum? Writing challenge using certain vocabulary? Foil boats? Foil boats that can carry the most weight? All of these activities could be recorded at home and shared in class, or even shared on the class website; and all (if not most) will keep students engaged in your curriculum long after the school day is over.

Consider giving a challenge over longer breaks. What about asking them to track how often they used technology versus talked with family members? How about tracking their eating habits when they're home? You can even use the bingo board to create challenges that will last one or two weeks. How about a photo-a-day challenge? Imagine all they'll have to share with the class when they return! Personally, I like the 30-Day Challenge presented by Matt Cutts in his TED Talk (ted.com/talks/matt_cutts_try_something_new_for_30_days). I've done this in December, prior to winter break. I modeled the challenge for my students by first brainstorming many ideas, pitching one to the class for feedback, and then sharing how I progressed. I then asked students to do the same—for twenty days. While they were in the midst of their challenge, I shared how I reflected on my twenty days, making sure I had some evidence to show for it (a chart, photos, video, etc.). They then shared the day prior to winter break. What better homework than encouraging students to set improvement goals? For twenty days they can work on their goals (no soda, no tech after 8 p.m., cook two new meals each week, exercise each day, read thirty minutes each day, learn something new each day, etc.) and track their results. Along the way, they can share their progress informally each week, then share with the class their success and struggles. In Chapter Nine, you'll see how this can be used to begin Genius Hour.

Reflection

It is possible that the very best type of homework is reflection. However, we need to give time during class for reflection. Could you possibly put aside five minutes every other day or so for students to reflect on what they know, what they struggle with, and where they'd like to be? Tack another few minutes on to this to allow time for them to share with peers in partners or small groups. Find the commonalities: Who succeeded in yesterday's work? Why? Use this time to also spot specific places where students struggle, and revisit those ideas in a mini lesson. What can those who succeeded teach the rest of the class to bring them further along? Instead of wondering, "Who hasn't done their homework?" we should be wondering, "Who doesn't understand the skill?" Use exit slips of some sort (sticky notes, charts, scrap paper, Google forms, etc.) for students to reflect on what they learned during the lesson, so you can better prepare for your next lesson!

Instead of wondering, "Who hasn't done their homework?" we should be wondering, "Who doesn't understand the skill?"

What if the student does not do the homework you're still assigning? Reflection is just as vital at this time. It's vital to find out the cause, especially if this child is a "repeat offender." Take the time to ask the child why he or she did not complete the work. If you do not have the actual time (Is it time to reconsider how you allocate time in class?), create a small piece of paper that fits in your pocket so it's easy to take out and hand to the child. It may have just three questions: Name, Assignment, and a simple "Why don't you have this assignment?" When you collect the sheet, the conversation can begin.

Reflection is the best type of homework for teachers as well. At the end of a lesson, jot down what went well, what you could have done to make it better, and other adjustments that need to be made. If it was particularly difficult, consider staff you might go to for advice. If a student was particularly helpful, send that "good note" home while he or she is on your mind. This type of homework for teachers is much more valuable than grading or even making sure plans for the next day are "perfect" (which you know they never really will be). After you reflect on your own, share some of your reflections with your students. Teach reflection by modeling the process—and the results.

What's In a Name?

Do you want your students to go home, knowing they have to do "work"? What if you offered homework, itself, as a choice? I've begun calling my homework "independent practice," because that's really what it is. Each morning, a student in my homeroom writes "Read for 20 minutes" under this heading. After first quarter, I've added a clear sheet protector with options for independent writing practice as well. These are kept on a document in Google Classroom so students can access them at any time. I will give feedback on these "extra" assignments. They do not count towards a grade. They are, as the title suggests, independent practice. So is the reading each night.

Have you tried to do the homework you assign each night? I am a reader, always keeping up with the newest children's literature and books for my own professional development. I tried, during my first 20-day challenge, to read for 30 minutes each night. Can you guess what happened? I did not read 30 minutes a night. Life got in the way! If I cannot do my own homework, is it fair to expect it of my students? Yes, I caught up most weekends, but I was thankful I didn't have a teacher checking it in for points each day. I would be stressed! My relationship with that teacher would probably be strained too—and I'm an adult!

Do you want your students to do more work when they get home from school? They've already spent seven hours (or more) working in school. If you read Alfie Kohn's work, you'll see the research about why it's bad practice to give typical homework (especially to elementary students). Home should offer some relaxation. It should be time to spend with family and friends. It should be time to help out in the house, or with the yard work. It should be time preparing for dinner, helping to fix a dessert, or chatting (or singing!) with siblings or a parent while they do the dishes. Add in sports, band, chess, and any other club you can think of, and there's hardly any time for more school work. So consider asking your students to do something at home—a challenge, an experiment, reading, writing, or a social skill. Do you still want to call it "homework"?

HOMEWORK GRADES

And here's the biggest shift. If you must assign homework, don't check it in. Don't put it in the gradebook. I've done it. I strongly believe not grading homework is the right thing to do. My students' scores on standardized tests have not taken a dive. If you want to assess achievement, why include practice (a.k.a. "homework") in the final grade? Completing practice work is a behavior. Behaviors don't belong in the gradebook. If students do not do homework, search for the reasons why. Ask the questions; don't punish with a zero. Adding a zero to an average is simply not fair. If you do not see the work, you cannot give it a grade. If anything, it should receive an "incomplete" or "missing" note, and this should be the catalyst for a discussion with the child.

Why, however, are you even collecting the homework if you've gotten this far? If you're giving challenges and independent practice, there is no reason to collect any of it. Feel free to ask about their "homework" in class, or even have them discuss it with a partner. Give feedback on what students did well (or have peers give feedback!) and where they could improve. Ask them to reflect on what they tried or learned. Then give coaching-type feedback to those who haven't tried yet that you'd love to see them grow as learners by doing the practice available to them. You might glean insights as to why they haven't done the work when you read their reflections. If not, begin that conversation, and get to the root of the matter. If you have middle or high school students, make sure that they know your class is just as important as the other classes, and should be given the same dedication, even though you are not collecting it or assigning a grade. The work is just as important, because it influences how much they learn. If students continue to refrain from completing any of the practice you assign, invite them in before school, during lunch, or after school to give them time to work on it. You can work while they work. (What a great role model!) Sometimes kids just need a dedicated time, a quiet space, and an adult who cares.

FURTHER READING

» Alfie Kohn, *The Homework Myth: Why our Kids Get Too Much of a Bad Thing* (Da Capo Life Long: 2006)

» Daniel T. Willingham, *Why Don't Students Like School? A Cognitive Scientist Answers Questions About How the Mind Works and What It Means for the Classroom* (Jossey-Bass: 2009)

» Jason Bretzmann, *Flipping 2.0: Practical Strategies for Flipping Your Class* (Bretzmann Group: 2013)

» Jocelyn K. Glei, "Take a Load Off: The Missing Key to Productivity Is Reflection" (jkglei.com/reflection/)

» John Spencer, "You Get Four Items and Forty-Five Minutes. What Will You Make?" (spencerauthor.com/2015/05/you-get-four-items-and-forty-five.html/)

» Sarah Schmalbruch, "Here's How Homework Differs Around the World" (thisisinsider.com/education-homework-differs-around-the-world-2016-11)

» Tom Wujec, "Instructions for Running a Marshmallow Challenge" (marshmallowchallenge.com/Instructions.html)

REFLECTION AND CALL TO ACTION

» Find out if your school or district has a policy about how much homework needs to go home, and begin the conversations about the value of homework with coworkers.

» Complete the work you assign. See how long each assignment takes, how much effort it requires, and then share this information with your students prior to assigning it. This may result in you tweaking (or tossing) the assignment prior to the students finding issues with it. Letting students know the approximate time it takes can reduce stress for them and may even lead to an exercise in time management.

» What worksheets do you give that could actually backfire if practiced incorrectly? Consider eliminating those. What kinds of activities could go on a choice board instead?

» What challenges could you give your students that would enhance your curriculum and also engage students enough that they'd want to share their progress when they come back to the classroom?

» Consider renaming the section on the board for homework, especially if you're not going to collect or grade it. What are some possible names you could try? Are you willing to ask students to choose from three that you like?

» What does "practice" mean? What are your thoughts on including practice in a student's final grade?

» List all the reasons you can think of as to why assignments
might not be completed and turned in on time. After you
list them, ask students—you can bet they'll have even more
reasons. Next, consider what the consequences should be.
Are there natural consequences? Are there also reasons you'd
consider as valid excuses? (Again, think of your own life and
when/why you don't complete certain things when you
expect to.)

_____

_____

_____

_____

_____

_____

_____

_____

_____

_____

_____

_____

7 Grading

"**H**ow many words does it have to be?"

"Will this be for a grade?"

"What's the point, if you're not going to grade it?"

"What can I do to bring up my grade?"

Grrrr. Questions like these irk the heck out of me. Why does so much revolve around a letter G-R-A-D-E?! It has taken me the past seven years to develop a mind shift to where I'm comfortable not talking about grades with students. Our focus is on *learning*. The words I choose to use revolve around the learning we're doing in class. Not the work. Not the lesson. And definitely not the grade. Last school year, I was able to pilot no grades with one of my three ELA classes. As a result, I pulled out my hair in my other two classes! Wait—I'm getting ahead of myself. Have I mentioned that these changes have taken me YEARS? I've changed things little by little. One step at a time. Sometimes I could only shift one aspect each year. But that's better than never changing at all, especially when I believe the shift is right for students. Before I go any further, I need to share a current anecdote:

S: Can I spend this time asking a peer for feedback on my narrative piece before I click "turn in"? [She's using Google Classroom.]

Me: Please do. Why don't you ask two peers, and ask them to focus on different aspects? Maybe one for "showing" with strong verbs and sensory details and another peer for grammar?

S: After I turn it in, can I use it for evidence for writing and grammar?

Me: If it's at least 200 words, and the feedback doesn't suggest you revise, then yes.

S: What if you just suggest a couple of revisions?

Me: You'll have to make that call. You'll want to use your three best pieces of evidence.

S: Will we have more time to write more pieces if I don't want to revise this piece again?

Me: We're four weeks in. I believe so. ;)

Remember the goal of this book is to help you make small shifts that will empower your students. What small shifts can you start tomorrow to make a difference when it comes to grading?

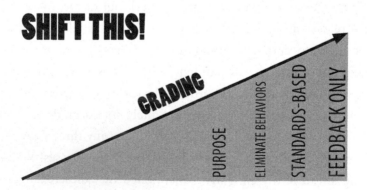

SHIFT WHAT YOU GRADE

Most educators and parents agree that the purpose of grades is to communicate student achievement. I remember going through my elementary school report card with my parents, seeing a lot of the letter "S" for "satisfactory" on many different skills. I was so proud that I shared with classmates and was kind. I believe I may have received an "NS" for "not satisfactory," as well, but of course I've blocked out the reason why! My parents knew how well I was doing in school based on myriad letters and hand-written comments. Throughout the years, many elementary schools have gone to one grade per subject—as a result of our automated grading system.

My questions regarding grading focus on their purpose: to communicate student achievement.

> » What is the purpose of school?

> » How long will teachers continue to give points to students who bring in boxes of tissues?

> » Why do I make all those comments if students just throw them in the trash?

> » Why should Erik be penalized for not doing any homework if he knows the material?

> » Why do my students have to know how old the Curtis boys (from *The Outsiders*) are?

> » Why don't my students revise their work?

Student questions also propel me towards changing my grading practices:

> » Can I redo this if I fail?

> » If I revise this assignment, what will my grade be?

» Why do I have to take grammar quizzes if my writing is good?

» How many points will it be off if I turn it in late?

Many ideas in this chapter may seem "too radical." But I know many teachers who are already successfully implementing these shifts. Before you read further, think of the purpose of school. I personally believe that school serves as a place for children to learn *with* and *from* one another and the community (teachers, parents, mentors invited in). It isn't to "get grades."

Some of my students have told me that the purpose of school is so you can go to college. Will grades help our students get into college? Perhaps—depending on the grades received and the college they'd like to attend. More colleges, however, are leaning towards evaluating portfolios for enrollment. And more students are choosing career paths that don't require a degree. Whatever you believe the purpose of school is, we should all agree it includes *learning*. And your students need to know that your goal is for them to *learn*. Learning could encompass the course material, how to get along with others, how to have a discussion, how and why to respect others, etc. Share this global concept of learning with your students during the first week of school and continue to use this language throughout the year. Your students won't be so grade-driven if your focus (and follow-through) revolves around learning.

So what is the purpose of grades within the context of learning? *The purpose of grades is to communicate student achievement.* If we keep this in mind as we consider what we're doing and why we're doing it, we'll be more critical of what we say and do in the classroom and in the gradebook. When you start thinking that these next few ideas are a bit radical, keep the purpose of grades in mind. Go ahead—highlight it! Then keep coming back to it as you progress through this chapter.

It's not about the grade.
It's about the learning.

Student Choice

Consider student choice before you read on. Imagine you're in science class, and your teacher has said, "Choose the portion of your report you'd like me to grade tonight" (claim, evidence, or reasoning). Perhaps you're in math, and your teacher has you choose three problems from your independent work that you'd like her to look at for a grade. Wouldn't you stop, reflect on and analyze your work, and perhaps revise a bit of it before you circle that portion (or those problems) to turn in for credit? When we're talking about grades, we're talking about achievement. Students will strive to achieve better when you give them time to reflect on what they did. Most often they know what their best work is, and they'll choose this work for feedback. It is not a stretch to ask very young students to do the same. This is not a shift in mindset when it comes to grading—this is simply asking students to reflect and giving them choice (while saving the teacher some time). Students will find their best work, and you will quickly know if they are on the right track or not.

Eliminate Behavior Points

Students should *not* receive points for bringing in a box of tissue to homeroom. Period. If students are not bringing in necessary supplies, it's time to change the way you ask for them. Small points add up, as we know, and students quickly become all too savvy regarding the tiny things they can do in order to bring up their overall grade. When we start calculating tiny points, our message is that it's about the grade rather than the *learning*. One of the things I love to say to my kids is, "It's not about the grade; it's about the learning!" (I even had a student paint this quote on a canvas and another had it sewn into a book bag for me. I think they're getting the message!)

Certain behaviors, such as bringing in supplies, filling in a worksheet, and/or being prepared with all materials, do not constitute learning. When points are a result of behaviors, there's something wrong with what we're doing. Those points simply show compliance and perhaps the ability to follow our directions. Yes, students can learn some lessons when practicing certain behaviors (especially if they become good habits), but there are better ways of encouraging these behaviors than handing out points.

It's time to get rid of these trivial points. This includes homework, extra credit, student behaviors, and pop quizzes. You read that right. Let's look at the reasons *why* as we dig into purpose.

Homework

What is the purpose of homework? In many instances, it's to *practice* what was taught in school. I addressed homework in the previous chapter, and I realize you may not be ready yet to stop giving homework. If this is the case, at least consider using homework as formative assessment. Consider the sports analogy: Practice after school is not graded—it's the game that counts. The games are the assessments. This is when the coach needs the players to succeed. My husband helped me realize this when we began geocaching. (Don't know about geocaching? Look it up! It's a great activity for families and school field trips!) We'd found two of the five caches we had planned to find. During a stop for air conditioning (in the local library, of course), we saw a student of mine with his father. I could tell he didn't want to talk. I figured it was because he was not happy with his grade. He was a reader, and I could tell this through his reading behaviors and through his writing. His grade was low because he turned in hardly anything to be graded.

It was wrong, and I explained it to my husband. He, in turn, compared our geocaching that day to a grade. Did I think we should get a 40 percent on our discoveries? Then why did I feel 100 percent when we found the "really tough" one? Looking for geocaches was practice. Finding one (or more) was achievement. And guess what? We used our failures to learn. Future geocaches were easier because of what we'd already practiced.

Use homework for the sole purpose of guiding your instruction. Keep track of it on a spreadsheet or even in your paper gradebook with a checkmark, but resist the urge to manage student behavior by attaching a grade. After all, we don't assign work because we're excited to go home and grade it. We're asking students to put forth the effort so they can learn the material as well as develop habits that will help them through life, such as prioritizing and time management. Will students still complete the homework? You will find that the students who completed the homework before grades were taken out of the equation will still do the homework. One problem I run up against is that if only one class is not grading homework (mine—I ask students to read at least twenty minutes each night) and other classes are grading it, students will do the other homework first, and may decide to skip the work I've assigned. After all, I'm not grading it, and they're still motivated by their other grades! I then put on my most serious face and say that "the homework I'm assigning will help you in every aspect of your life, or I would not ask you to do it. Reading will give you an advantage in life." I truly believe this is the case in my class. (Of course, most middle school or high school teachers believe their subject is the "most important." We are a passionate breed.)

If students are not doing the homework, find out the cause instead of punishing them with poor marks. If you're tracking the behavior with checkmarks in an online gradebook, parents and students who check grades will see the information. After a student hasn't turned in more than you're comfortable with, it's time to have a conversation.

Consider the following reasons students don't complete and turn in their homework:

» The homework is too difficult (they need more guidance).

» The homework is too easy (especially if they've mastered that particular skill).

» They can't get online (consider having a paper version accessible).

» They get "Bs" in class because their test scores are out of this world. Do they even need homework?

» They have myriad activities after school.

» They do other homework first.

» They aren't getting any sleep.

» They take care of the household.

» They think it won't help them.

» They think it's a "hassle" (true story!).

» Or worst of all, they practice it wrong each night and have stopped trying altogether.

Having that discussion with the student will go a long way for both of you. Approach the issue respectfully in a calm manner. Doing so will let the child know you care, and it will alert the child that you assign the work because you believe it is important and beneficial.

Remember: Learning skills is the goal. Helping students understand that learning (rather than a grade) is the ultimate goal will build more trust than any punishment of a missing mark in the gradebook would.

 Remember:
Learning skills is the goal.

Extra Credit

You've been there. The scenario: "Jenny" has a C+ going into the last week of the quarter. "Can I do extra credit?" she inquires. Just say no. Don't do it! You will be giving in to all the grade-grubbers in the world if you do. You will be perpetuating a system that regards grades as more important than the learning. If students want to "get a better grade," they should be revising or redoing the work that you originally designed to help them learn. While you're shifting things, shift your vocabulary from getting good grades to doing better in class. If the work assigned is not something you'd let them redo in order to learn, it's time to assess the relevance of the work you're assigning! If they do not have the grade they want, it is because they haven't learned the material—yet. In order to learn the material, they need to complete what the class has already done to the best of their ability. Only then will the learning occur.

But wait! The presidential debates are on this week! My students should get credit for watching them, because they'll learn from them! No. Find another way to motivate students to watch a show that's on television, a movie related to your content that happens to be at the theaters, or to visit the museum downtown. On the night of said documentary, set up a backchannel where students can talk about the event. This can be as simple as making a Google Doc ahead of time that all students can access from home. Or use TodaysMeet. Or have them post to their Twitter or Instagram accounts using a specific hashtag. If you have younger students, have them draw what they notice and come back to share in class the next day. But do not give extra credit. If a student sits through a show or walks through an exhibit, it does not guarantee that he or she has learned anything. Keep the purpose of what a grade should mean in mind. The purpose of a grade is to communicate student achievement. Extra credit for extra work (not necessarily progress or achievement) only confuses the issue of what the final grade means.

STUDENT BEHAVIORS

Homework and extra credit are considered work that students do. "Doing" does not necessarily mean "learning." There are a few student behaviors that teachers add to the grade book, thinking they will help their students develop better habits, but these behaviors should not be included in student achievement. What behaviors should we keep track of but keep separated from the overall grade? Participation, punctuality, and neatness.

Participation

Participation in class can be tallied if you're organized enough. Tally student questions, comments, insights, collaboration, and even blurt outs. Keep this record and use it as a basis for discussion with students. After I read *Hacking Education* by Mark Barnes and Jennifer Gonzalez, I came up with this track record—tinyurl.com/ShiftTrackRecords—so I can keep track of behaviors such as participation. I am open and honest about it with students, and they know that I carry a clipboard around with me to keep track of things. This record leads to constructive discussions with students about their positive, helpful participation, and it also helps me see who is not participating, or who gets us off track at times. Showing students your tallies helps them see that it's not a judgment. It's an observation. It is then time to set goals for the next week or so. This is all done without assigning a single mark to it. Find out how your online grading system works. What's worked for me is putting these behaviors into the online system as comments only. (For example, when I look at our tracking sheet for the week and I want to communicate regarding "being prepared for class," I copy/paste this type of comment in the gradebook: *Came to class prepared with reading material each day but one this week.* This does not affect the grade. Instead, it helps parents and their children have the conversation about what that particular comment means. It is that conversation that helps promote certain behaviors in the classroom. Tracking in this way also helps me to stay positive with "repeat offenders." If one student is late to class, I do not harp on her that day. Instead, I wait for a few days to pass to make sure it wasn't a one-time thing. If the tardiness continues, I can then show her the record of my observations.

Punctuality

Punctuality with schoolwork is a habit that we'd like to encourage as well. I accept work at any point up until I'm finished giving feedback to all other students. If it's still not in front of me by the time I'm done looking at all other students' work, I do not give a zero for that assignment. If you're averaging marks for a final grade, a zero is very detrimental and virtually impossible for students to overcome! After one or two, students feel (and it is most likely true!) that they cannot recover from them, so why shouldn't they continue not doing the work? Why not take the easy way out? Making sure students stay in with you to do the work is more of a punishment to them than the zero—and it actually helps them learn. Let's make it difficult for students to fail—it is our responsibility. We want each child to succeed!

I cannot, in good conscience, let a student earn a zero. Nor can I take "points off" for each day an assignment is late. I wouldn't get any sleep! I know adults who are late many times, and yet they still show up and do their job once they've arrived. When a student turns in an assignment late, I put a symbol in the gradebook, alerting the student that it has not been turned in ("I" for "incomplete" or "M" for "missing"). Next, I ask that student to either work on it before school, during lunch, or after school with me present. This typically works, and then I can give feedback to that student in the moment, remembering to inquire as to why the work was late (and set a goal for the next assignment). If tardiness is an issue, tally the instances, and ask the student why there is a pattern. If that doesn't work, contact the parents. Punctuality is not something you should grade.

What about long-term absences? When children are absent from school, their missing work piles up. This is when you need to evaluate what you think is most necessary for students to complete in order to learn the material missed, and what could be dismissed for the moment, as this child is already behind. (If attendance issues persist, direct families to absencesaddup.org for help getting their child to school.)

Neatness

When it comes to neatness, I'd love to work in the lower grades. So much of the mess is acceptable! My writing drafts are incomprehensible to anyone but me, and that's acceptable as well. Each year I try to make more and more of the work I assign relevant to students—this helps them work more diligently on the neatness of their assignment. If work being submitted is not neat "enough" for me to understand the student's message, I'll ask the student to redo it and submit it again for more feedback. The lesson learned by needing to redo the assignment usually deters the student from turning in a similar piece again.

Who will be looking at the assignment/product? Is it solely the teacher? Students may not need to redo assignments when there is an authentic audience—they will be motivated by knowing there is an audience other than you! This is yet another reason to make sure your assignments are relevant. Perhaps students can publish their assignment on a blog post, poster, pamphlet, or product that other students, parents, or other community members may see. When there is an audience for the work (other than the teacher), children will work harder and want to display neater work. I stress to students that if their work is not neat or edited, their readers (or viewers) may not get the message they intended. If it is not legible, what will be the result? Mistakes and sloppy work deter from the message—in any subject matter. This works if their audience is someone other than their teacher. There will be no need to give a mark for "neatness," nor should there be if we're providing students with work that is meaningful and relevant to them.

If we believe that the purpose of an overall grade is to communicate student achievement, then behaviors such as participation, punctuality, and neatness should not be taken into account.

POP QUIZZES

Surprising students deflates any trust you've built up with your class. Teachers often give pop quizzes to see if their students read the material the night before. Or perhaps to see if they've been studying along the way. School should not be a place to play a game of "gotcha." Playing this game sabotages the trust students have in you. This, to me, sounds like what I might call a "comprehension check." These have no business being included in a student's overall grade. If the grade is used to show achievement, why include checks for comprehension along the journey? Sports game scores are not based on the practices players have had up until then. We need to give students room to learn from failure, not punish them. If you must give a pop quiz, ask students to reflect on the results, set a goal for next time, and then keep any score far away from the gradebook.

SHIFT TO STANDARDS-BASED GRADING

So what *do* you put in the gradebook? What is "worthy enough" of being included to demonstrate student achievement? It's true that you may have fewer marks in the gradebook than ever before. This should be fine, as long as you're allowing for redos and retakes. Here's the shift that leads us to standards-based grading. I see standards-based grading as grading for *achievement only*—the way grading is supposed to be. It resembles the report cards I would get in elementary school: excellent, satisfactory, not satisfactory, and not applicable (at this time).

Collect Evidence

The first step in this shift is to only include work that shows evidence of learning the standards. Schools designate four numbers in this type of marking system. A score of a "4" might mean "mastery." A "3" might mean "proficient." A "2" could mean "developing," and a "1" could mean "needs improvement." I've seen other categories being used, such as "meets standard," "approaching standard," and even "not there yet."

I've been there. I've tried it—with a typical letter grade report card. Here's what worked and what didn't: At first, parents were upset because they saw a mark of a "2" looking like it was 50 percent. This makes sense when you look at it as if it is a grade out of four points. After all, the computer calculated it for us! A "3," then, was a 75 percent, and teachers in our ELA department did not like to give 75 percent or 50 percent for work. It was very uncomfortable, and many of us felt it was unkind as well. Our quick fix was to change the percentages of these numbers. (Keep in mind that we were averaging these out for one final letter grade at the end.) Since "proficient" to us meant "A" work, we assigned a "3" to mean 90 percent. The "2" became 75 percent, and the "1" became 50 percent. Students, parents, and teachers alike felt more comfortable with this system, even though this was not standards-based grading by any means.

We were also on board with letting students revise their work for a better mark. If they took our suggestions into account, it was possible, and we felt students were actually becoming more skilled with their work. However, it was still a mark, and students were still playing the numbers game. Why should they think of revising the work with a "1," when revising the "2" would be much easier and a quicker shot at an "A"?!

The problem with including standards-based grading and using these four numbers is when you come to the end of the grading period.

What then? You cannot, and should not, average these numbers. Averaging distorts the message—big time. It just doesn't work if you are trying to translate these scores into one letter grade. A true standards-based grading system reports out on each standard and does not average these marks into one final letter grade.

How do we fix this if we must report out one grade at the end of the grading period? How do we work within the system we're given? Check out the next step because we're on our way to the last and largest shift when it comes to grading.

Most Current Evidence

The final grade isn't an average. It is simply a final grade to communicate what the student knows. If we want to show student achievement, we don't want to include what the student *used to know*. We only want to report out to parents, next year's teachers, etc. what the student knows at that moment. Let's say your child is ready to ride a bicycle. When he finally gets it, it discounts all the falling over and time in training wheels he's had up until then. He can ride that bike! We need to collect a lot of evidence of learning various standards. When one standard is mastered consistently by a student, he shouldn't need to do much more work on that one—he's got it! A check-in every now and then is appropriate, but he needs to spend more time working on the standards in which he struggles. I am excited for the day my own district moves to standards-based grading.

How can teachers work within the constraints of one letter grade per grading period? Choose the most current evidence you have on each standard. You'll still be forced to mesh these into one grade, but a printout of each standard and student progress would be beneficial to attach to the report so students, parents, and future teachers have more information about student achievement. Until your school is reporting each standard separately, using current evidence only to come up with one letter grade works better than averaging all the marks together.

Feedback Only

By now, you have hopefully realized that one letter grade for a subject is a bogus concept. What does it tell us about what the student has achieved? An "A" in math? Does that mean that she can use the right formulas in certain situations? Does that mean that he knows how to multiply fractions? Since grades are so arbitrary, and each teacher calculates them differently, what's to stop us from not giving any marks at all? Granted, it may be decades from now before digital portfolios totally replace letter grades, but we can work within the system.

Paul Black and Dylan Wiliam make a strong case for feedback in lieu of marks. (See *Inside the Black Box* listed in the Further Reading section of this chapter.) In their research, they found that the students who improved were those who were only given feedback or comments on their work. No mark was attached. If feedback was given and a mark was attached, there was no improvement in student work. Have you seen this phenomenon? You comment on a student's work, giving stellar suggestions for improvement, put the mark on the top, and hand it back. The student sees the mark and then tosses it in the "circular file." The learning stopped when he turned in the assignment. You wonder about the time you invested looking at each student's work. We need to stop placing judgment on student work, and make it about *improving* the work instead. I'm done giving marks. I piloted this idea with one class in 2015, and now I cannot go back. The year I tested this idea, I decided to give video feedback for students' writing. I spent approximately five minutes screencasting my feedback, then I uploaded it to YouTube and copied the unlisted link to the online gradebook. I did all this—only to find out students never watched the video feedback! Why not? Because on their rubrics, I still highlighted where their skills fell. I was *still giving marks*. So the learning *stopped when they saw the mark*. I still share the rubrics with students—to show our goals for each skill—but I do not mark it on their work. I give narrative feedback only.

Check out **tinyurl.com/ShiftGrading** for a video explaining how my seventh grade ELA classes are currently functioning without marks. For more ideas on how to give feedback, tools for feedback, teachers' journeys with this type of learning, and more go to **tinyurl.com/FeedbackBinder.**

Quality Feedback

When you decide to go this route, one thing you and your students must work on is quality feedback. Quality feedback is timely, above all. Feedback is more effective when given very soon after the task. Make sure to include time in your lessons for teacher (one-on-one, group, or whole-class) and peer (partner or group) feedback.

Feedback should also be specific. Before you give students feedback, have them give you feedback. Go through a math problem (writing prompt, developing a hypothesis, etc.) on the projector, thinking aloud as you go, and when you're finished, ask students to tell you what, specifically, you did well. This should eliminate the "great job" and "I liked it" comments. You may want to give them feedback starters, such as "I like how you _____. It showed me _____."

Next, ask them to give you suggestions for improvement. Paul Solarz, a fifth grade teacher and author of *Learn Like a Pirate*, calls these "quality boosters." We've used this term in our classes, and the kids take it to heart. They enjoy helping one another improve their work. Once students give you feedback, put up student work from a prior class or prior year. Demonstrate to students how to give quality boosters in a respectful way. Again, consider starters:

» "What would happen if you _____ instead?"

» "Consider _____."

» "Have you thought about _____?"

Now it's time for students to practice with one another. Set up partnerships for students to show their work. Remind students that this is non-judgmental. It should be task focused. It's all about helping them improve. Even masters at their craft want to improve! Walk around the room, jotting down words you hear that are encouraging, non-judgmental, and helpful. When students are finishing, share these specific words with students, and ask them why they think you chose to share them.

There is one last step in helping students give one another strong feedback: Ask if any students will be courageous enough to share their own thinking. Make sure you are sharing models of teacher feedback before you expect students to give feedback to one another. You need to model this for students. The more students share their writing with the class for whole-class and teacher feedback, the more students will feel comfortable doing so. Be sure to repeat this practice often.

One reason to dedicate a lot of time guiding peer feedback is that you want to incorporate a *lot* of feedback if you're not giving out marks. The more feedback students can give one another before you see their polished work, the better the work will be by the time it gets to you. You can then give feedback on more challenging aspects of their work, enabling you to push your students further.

> The more feedback students can give one another before you see their polished work, the better the work will be by the time it gets to you.

One piece of advice I need to add comes from Peter Johnston's book, *Choice Words*. When guiding students in how to give feedback, explain that the word "but" is off limits. If you say something positive about student work, then follow up with "but," you contradict the first part of what you said. If you want to say something positive about student work, say it (or write it) by itself. Then give the quality booster separately, and make it a choice for students to change it or not. It is their work—they own it. You can coach them, encouraging them to try different things, and then they have to make the decision to take your advice or not. You won't always be there to hold their hands. Make sure they know that they can take the feedback and run with it to see if it makes their work stronger, or they can ignore it. If they choose to ignore it, they still have the option of revisiting it later. Let the students know, either way, that you have very high standards for them, and you know they can meet those standards.

How does this work in primary grades? Take six minutes to check out lessons young ones can learn from "Austin's Butterfly" —tinyurl.com/ShiftButterfly. (*Hint: This video works with many grades, as students see the simplicity and value of feedback!*)

Feedback is pointless if a student never acts on it. Therefore, be sure you provide time in class for students to look over (or listen to) their feedback and then act on it right away. Revision might not happen if you assign it to be completed after school, and feedback is much more effective when it's taken into account in a timely manner instead of at a later date.

The more specific, skill-directed feedback you provide, the more skilled you will become at giving even stronger feedback that will encourage growth. This language will then permeate your school day. Your students will begin to mimic the language as well. (And you will dance—and perhaps sing—in the hallways!) It will take time, but one day you will notice how your language has changed. You'll most likely become aware of the change when speaking with teachers who are not on the same page as you when it comes to grading. You'll hear "points," "extra credit," zeroes," and "no more redos or retakes." You'll have to remember that you are at a different place, and then remember all the changes you've made up until now as well. If you want them to understand more, take the time to share with them the reasons *why* you made the shift.

Reflection

Reflection is vital. It's part of the process of learning. After peer feedback and teacher feedback, give time for students to reflect. Some may choose to revise their work; others may not. Either way, ask students to reflect—orally, in pairs, on paper, etc.—on what they've decided to do, and why. Feel free to give them leads here as well, as they may not be used to reflection exercises. Some questions to ask include the following:

> » "What did I learn?"
>
> » "What does it mean?"
>
> » "Now what? What are my next steps?"

INVOLVE STUDENTS FURTHER

Here is where the feedback and reflection come together to create the overall grade. You and/or your students need to decide where you're going to keep the evidence, feedback, and reflections you generate. Digital portfolios are an option, as are simple binders or folders. Once the evidence is collected, it's time to look for consistency. Consistent evidence is what will help you determine a final grade for the grading period. It's best to do this while sitting right alongside students.

This may mean, as Mark Barnes says in *Assessment 3.0*, that you have to put aside four hours or so in the last week of the grading period to meet with students. One way around the time issue with older students is to give them the task of putting the evidence together themselves, then sharing with you in a written or video reflection. You can read or watch this ahead of time, and only meet with students you may disagree with. I'm of the mindset, however, that even if you disagree, give the student the grade he believes he deserves. If you do not, then the focus is put back on the grade, and not the learning. Still have the discussion about the reasons why you disagree, and put emphasis on the value of honest reflection. Then help these students set goals for the next grading period. You can send these goals home with their grade report and use them to help the student assess himself more accurately the next time around. One work-around for a class of younger students would be collecting their evidence for them and giving them your thoughts about their achievement a couple of weeks prior to the end of each grading period. If students feel differently, give them a chance to support their claims.

What constitutes each letter grade is probably the toughest decision when you're only dealing with feedback. When it comes to math, you may be able to take the five or so most recent scores on tasks if they're consistent, or you may decide that averaging the last five or so tasks works best for each standard. I still struggle with how to come up with a final grade, as it is somewhat arbitrary—albeit less than past practices. But get this—the students help me. Because we include so much reflection, most of them have a good handle on where they are and where they are heading. Have these discussions with students ahead of time. Some will be harder on themselves than you would—and just as many would be easier on themselves! Collaborative reflection and grading will be a new idea for them as well, and some may struggle with it as much as you. It's better to figure it out with the students throughout the grading period than to not know when it's time to have a final end-of-grading-period conference. Involving students in these decisions will create buy-in and trust, which will go a long way when it comes to their motivation to learn.

I can sense teachers of older students still thinking, *They won't work if there's no grade attached.* They will. They will, not only to be able to provide evidence at the end of each grading period, but because you've modified the culture in the classroom to one that is about helping one another learn and improve. I truly believe this. My students prove it to me every day.

FINAL THOUGHTS

I'll probably never have "final thoughts" on the subject of grading. Long after this book is published and I've done more research, I'll want to add more. I feel the shifts toward "healthier grading" are vital if we want to cultivate a culture of learning. Some teachers prefer percentages and marks in the gradebook. I know I used to. It was much easier than what I'm doing now! There are books listed in the Further Reading section below for you to read and highlight. The experts and their supporting research will convince you that this shift in grading truly is the right thing to do—along with making work relevant and meaningful to our children. I lean on the experts' words often—to share with students, parents, and other teachers.

It has taken me years to adjust my own thinking, grading procedures, and language I use regarding learning. I will be learning still for years to come. I've failed many students along the way when I graded every little thing, and when many of my assignments were given simply because "I don't have enough grades in the gradebook yet." (Thank goodness I've shifted my teaching!) I now include more instances of feedback each quarter in the gradebook than I've ever had of actual grades! I feel like I'm finally being more fair to and respectful of my students now that I've been through so many shifts in my own thinking. It's a ton of hard work. I'm not doing it because I think it's easier or even fun; I'm changing the system with my own students because I believe it will better prepare them for life. I don't want children to be motivated by carrots and sticks, rewards and punishments, or numbers and letters. I want them to strive for improvement. I want them to love learning for learning's sake. Another reason I'm changing the system is because this system helps me improve each lesson. If I expect students to be able to give proof that they are learning, all of my lessons need to revolve around relevant tasks that focus on the standards I need to teach.

I wonder how many more shifts I'll have when it comes to giving feedback in lieu of grading. My lessons, feedback, and reflections are far from perfect. It's been a very long process for me, because I've tried it alone. Have the conversations with coworkers, parents, and students. Keep asking the hard questions and always go back to what is best for kids and helpful to developing a mindset geared toward lifelong learning.

FURTHER READING

» Alfie Kohn, "From Degrading to De-Grading" (*High School Magazine*: March 1999)

» Cathy Vatterott, *Rethinking Grading: Meaningful Assessment for Standards-Based Learning* (ASCD: 2015)

» Feedback In Lieu of Grades Livebinder: tinyurl.com/ FeedbackBinder

» Joe Bower, "My De-Grading Philosophy Q & A" (joebower.org/ 2011/05/my-grading-philosophy-q.html)

» John Hattie and Helen Timperly, "The Power of Feedback" (*Review of Educational Research*: 2011)

» Ken O'Connor, *A Repair Kit for Grading: 15 Fixes for Broken Grades* (Pearson: 2011)

» Mark Barnes, *Assessment 3.0: Throw Out Your Grade Book and INSPIRE Learning* (Corwin: 2015)

» Paul Black and Dylan Wiliam, *Inside the Black Box: Raising Standards Through Classroom Assessment* (Learning Sciences International: 2011)

» Paul Solarz, *Learn Like a Pirate: Empower Your Students to Collaborate, Lead, and Succeed* (Dave Burgess Consulting: 2015)

» Peter H. Johnston, *Choice Words: How Our Language Affects Children's Learning* (Stenhouse: 2004)

» Rick Wormeli, *Fair Isn't Always Equal* (Stenhouse: 2006)

» Thomas R. Guskey, "Five Obstacles to Grading Reform" (*Educational Leadership:* Nov 2011)

REFLECTION AND CALL TO ACTION

» Check an old gradebook of yours, if you've still got it. If not, make up a fake one. Add in random marks (percentages, letters) for assignments you usually mark. Now average the scores for each student. Who is the "C" student, and why? What makes an "A" student in your class? Start to notice averages, and see what types of stories they tell. What would parents get out of just one letter grade at the end of each grading period?

» Where are you asking for compliance instead of learning? Look through the rubrics and grades you typically use, and see where you can cut points that do not show achievement.

» What, if anything, do you feel is wrong with the way you or your colleagues are grading? If you know something is wrong with your current system, how long will it be before you feel ready to make adjustments? Set a date as a goal, and put it on your to-do list.

» Choose something from the Further Reading section above or look online for videos from Rick Wormeli or presentation slides from Ken O'Connor. Check it out with a colleague. Have the conversations that will help your students succeed.

_____

_____

_____

_____

8 | Social Media

It's all about figuring out what your choices are and trying to make the right ones.

—*The Other Boy* by M.G. Hennessey

I created a Twitter account in August of 2011. I'd used the account once, on opening day that year, at the request of our principal. He asked us for three words to guide us through the coming school year. I remember a co-worker's quote: "Optimism overcomes obstacles." I loved Julie Kunst's quote, and I still take it to heart today. And that was where my Twitter experience ended.

UNTIL ... fast forward six months. I'm at a workshop my district sent me to in Michigan. Ewan McIntosh (from Scotland!) is leading it, and it's fabulous. (In fact, here is where my journey with Genius Hour began—we worked on a problem we had in our own school!) At the end of the workshop, he suggested we follow the hashtag for the workshop to keep in touch and help one another succeed at our action research. Wha?? I had no clue what he was talking about, so I asked a peer. She showed me that, on Twitter, you could "follow" a hashtag. "The number sign?" I asked. Yup. I went home, looked at these things called hashtags, and suddenly I was hooked.

Twitter is for celebrities! Twitter is for athletes! Twitter is for people who want to share pictures of their meals! Yes … and most definitely … absolutely *not*. Twitter, like other online social media tools, is what you make of it. Here were my questions when I considered social media—for learning's sake:

> » Isn't (insert social media tool here) just for Justin Bieber?
>
> » Who uses it?
>
> » Why would teachers use it?
>
> » Who can see what I post?
>
> » What if my students follow me?
>
> » What if parents of my students follow me?
>
> » What if my administration follows me??!!
>
> » Why would anyone want to see what I post?
>
> » How do you use it?
>
> » How can I get something from using it?

And guess what? I was *scared* of using any social media tool. My family was on Facebook, and I stayed very far away from it. I heard horror stories and knew so many things could go wrong! I got on Twitter because my principal asked me to, but I was not going to say anything on there that wasn't required of me. I most definitely was not going to say anything that wasn't related to teaching.

SHIFT TO CONNECTION

That was then. *Now* I'm writing to help you overcome your fear of social media. Even when I speak at conferences where technology is the focus, I proclaim, "It's not about the tech! It is because of the technology that we can make connections." Making the connections can help us learn more when it comes to our profession. Do you feel like you already know enough? *Nah*—you wouldn't be reading this! You're one of the teachers who knows we need to continue learning in order to be the best for our students. Attending one conference a year just doesn't cut it. Reading one professional book isn't enough. Imagine if the person who styles your hair never learned about new techniques or fashions. You'd be walking around with a beehive or a bowl cut! Imagine if your doctor didn't learn from other doctors' experiences. They'd still be using leeches, and patients would run in the other direction! I have grown leaps and bounds in my teaching because of what I've learned as a result of connecting with others using social media tools. I have also learned how to be a better communicator, and I continue to attempt to transfer these skills to my students. I am excited each morning to see what else I can learn from my PLN (professional learning network). Put your seatbelt on—once you begin this ride, you will experience many thrills!

Lurk and Learn

Most of my references are regarding the tool we call Twitter, but I'll let you know that I've now used Instagram, Facebook, Snapchat, and Voxer to connect with teachers, other classes, and my own students (depending on the tool). I often wonder how many more tools there will be by the time I retire! You can apply these tips to many tools.

Here's a secret that many people new to these tools don't know: You don't have to "follow" *anyone*. It's true. You can lurk, and it's not even considered creepy! (Feel free to call this stage "exploring," if that suits you better.)

One way teachers can lurk is through the use of hashtags. A hashtag is a category of sorts. I began by lurking on #edchat. On this particular hashtag, you'll find teachers of all sorts—every grade level, every subject, educators, and administrators. After typing in a hashtag in the "search" option of the tool, just watch, and refresh the page. After you watch for a bit, click around. Click on links shared, user names, and other hashtags used in each post. Do some exploring.

Exploring is where the learning takes place; it's where the magic happens! You will soon find yourself reading blog posts, reviews of books, and research articles. You'll find online tools you can use with your students, teachers who teach what you teach, questions you should be asking yourself, live streams of speakers at conferences you are not even paying to attend, videos that inspire and make you cry and cheer, answers you've been looking for but didn't even know it, and ideas you'll want to use in your class the *very next day*. And if this isn't enough, perhaps most importantly, you'll find educators from around the world who love to share what they are learning, every day, twenty-four hours a day, seven days a week. *Oooh!* One more thing. Get this: It's *free!*—a teacher's dream!

Exploring is where the learning takes place; it's where the magic happens!

I have found many free tools to use as well. Share these tools with your students: tinyurl.com/KirrTech. I created this document because my first summer on Twitter, my feed was flooded with tech tools, and it was a bit too much for me to handle. I wanted to try all of them out all summer long! Instead, I created a spreadsheet (that is constantly evolving) and now I share it with my students. They, in turn, use the tools for their presentations, projects, studying, and fun! They have even taught me how to use some of the tools. It is because of social media that my students and I can learn new tools together.

Share and Connect

After you get over the *awesomeness* of lurking and learning, you'll soon get the urge to ask questions. It's time to step out and connect with one or two people. Most educators who use social media are, or have been, in your place at one time or another and shared your perspective. They understand you. They've been there.

Reach out! Ask a question about something they've posted. Ask for more about the topic they're sharing. Teachers who use social media *love* to share what they've tried that has been successful, and they love to guide you to other resources they've discovered. If there's no one in particular you'd like to ask your question to, use a hashtag to categorize it. Search online for "educational hashtags," and you'll see too many to count. People (*ahem*—like me) scour certain hashtags for ideas, and if they see your question and can help, you'll receive an answer. Keep that person on your radar, so you can connect and learn from him or her again at a later date. The more connections you make, the more people you'll see that can be your "marigolds"—people who help you thrive in your workplace. This leads right into collaboration, which is a crucial goal of teachers who want to grow!

Collaborate and Change

You've begun sharing ideas you've found online. Others are now sharing your ideas. Suddenly, someone adds to an idea you've shared. Yes. Adds to it. You're stunned—why didn't you think of that?! Now you're rockin'. You thank the contributor, and you jump into adding it to what you're already doing. It happens. All the time! Those same educators who share what they're doing are using your ideas and making them better—for you! It's as if you've got the best, most collaborative teachers at your fingertips.

Here's one example of how I've collaborated with teachers I've never met: Robert Kaplinsky (from California, USA) wrote a blog post that was getting retweeted many times over (robertkaplinsky. com/observeme/) regarding a simple way to invite other teachers to observe your lessons. It came across my feed, and I thought that I'd like to have other teachers come into my room, observe me, and give me feedback on specific skills. The template he used was a Word document, and I wanted to use a Google presentation, as I don't have much access to Word anymore. I created my own, and added a QR (quick response) code to a form I made so teachers could give digital feedback if they wanted. I put the invite outside the door to our classroom this year, then I tweeted the photo (using the hashtag #ObserveMe). Teachers began retweeting my photo, and it was only two days later when another teacher, Laurel Beaton (from Alberta, Canada), shared that she'd love for people to observe the way her students were working together! Of course, I soon created another version of the sign outside our door. Other teachers have since put their own spins (and decorations!) on this simple idea, and have shared them using the same hashtag. What a stellar idea to help teachers grow and learn from one another—if they take the opportunity to come in and visit.

Collaborating with "real" people you've never met will lead you to actually meet these fabulous educators. You can lurk for only so long before it's time to meet in person. While I was first learning about hashtags, I found #sschat, which is for social studies teachers. (I didn't know this at the time.) I was in awe of how the tweets just kept coming. One person was posing questions, while so many others were answering the questions and "chatting" with one another. Amazed, I remember sitting at my kitchen table in silence, not touching the computer as I watched the tweets fly. I knew there was never going to be a time when I could ever participate—how wrong I was!

At some point during the "conversation," Shawn McCusker (who, I learned, taught in a neighboring district) invited participants to what he called #EdCampOshkosh. I had no clue what it was. I later found out it was an "EdCamp" in Oshkosh, Wisconsin. EdCamps are "organic, participant-driven professional learning experiences" (edcamp.org). What are EdCamps—really? EdCamps are my Disneyland. EdCamps are where I can kibitz with teachers who are just as passionate about teaching as I am. EdCamps do not have a schedule. In this one-day format, participants set the schedule. They suggest what they want to share or learn about, and then go to those sessions that work for them. I did attend the EdCamp in Oshkosh that summer, the first of so many I've lost count. Shawn McCusker was there that day, and he tweeted me a photo of his shirt before I got started that morning so I could sit by him. Mustering up my courage to sit with a "stranger," I looked for him, and he recognized me. He welcomed me to sit and began to share how excited he was about being there. I went to two fifty-minute sessions, ate lunch at the table where EdCamp Madison was dreamed of and conceived, and then I had to take a break from the third of four sessions, because my brain was on information overload! EdCamps are where you meet your tribe. The use of a social media tool led me to making *personal* connections with local educators. My husband and I often take mini-weekend vacations so I can attend in a neighboring state!

Connecting and collaborating with passionate educators—local and worldwide—will change your thinking. I've often heard (and believe!) that Twitter is a teacher's favorite teachers' lounge. There are more suggestions and questions than there are complaints! Instead of complaining, these people act! The more you learn from them, the more you realize you do NOT know. Your vocabulary will grow, and your word choice will be more precise (as there is only so much physical room to write using social media venues). I now call my students scholars, researchers, writers, readers, mathematicians, scientists, explorers, etc., depending on the activity. I have learned how to make my message more effective by using fewer characters. My language (spoken and written) has become more precise. (Imagine how much students can learn about communication if they are only allowed 140 characters at a time!) Using social media has kept me up to date with what's changing in education. I want to be on that wagon, and even hold the reins sometimes! Being active on social media has helped me (and those I share with) build a culture of collaboration and inquiry. If we want students to be inquisitive, collaborative, and communicate effectively, we should model these behaviors. Just recently, one teacher asked others on Twitter to share why they tweet. Mike Stein (@mike_stein33) answered, "I tweet because the synergistic swapping of great ideas with enthusiastic teachers has rejuvenated my career" (Nov 23, 2016). *Yes!* Learning from others using social media is rejuvenating!

Connecting and collaborating with passionate educators—local and worldwide—will change your thinking.

Reflecting on Learning

When you get to this stage of connecting and collaborating, you may want to begin blogging. The practice of sharing your ideas and questions in blog format is very reflective. In order to blog, you need to organize your thoughts on the subject. Doing that alone—without even clicking "publish"—is reflection itself! Once someone shares or comments on a post of yours, you'll be hooked and will want to blog even more. I often look back at older posts and reflect on how things have changed since I wrote them, or I'm reminded why I chose one way over another. Blogging is one great way to connect, collaborate with others, and change your vision. Think of it as your journal or your action research. Document your reflections so you and others can learn from them.

Occasionally an educator will question an idea you've shared on your blog. Sometimes they're playing devil's advocate, or they may actually be disagreeing with the idea. Here's where a growth mindset can benefit you. You can either choose not to communicate with that person anymore (you can learn how to easily block certain people), or you can follow his or her lead and question the idea yourself. I find that I grow more when my ideas are questioned. It forces me to take a step back and reflect on what I really believe and what I want to say or share. Why did I share it in the first place? What was the value I found in it? Is it really something I believe? Why do I believe in it? Being challenged by other educators has motivated me to be more clear in my word choice. I've taken more time to think before I share—which is a skill to learn when you're sharing on social media. Fancy that. Using social media has helped me to become more effective at using social media. Hence one of the reasons for the last shift in this chapter—getting the students involved!

Involve Your Students

Remember the fears you had getting on social media for yourself? Why in the world would you want your students on it?! Because using social media helps people become more effective at using social media. Our students will use it. Maybe not today. Maybe not this year. But they will use it when they can, and we can be role models that help them use it in a positive fashion.

Let me take a moment to revisit my questions when I was wondering if I, personally, should use social media. I'll include answers this time:

Q: Isn't (insert social media tool here) just for Justin Bieber?

A: No. Sure, he's on it. Sure, my students may follow celebrities, but I don't have to.

Q: Who uses it?

A: Most anyone with a smartphone over a certain age and under a certain age. (I don't know this statistic, and each tool is different.) Some of my students follow me on Instagram. A couple of times I've used it as a tool to get a few of them to come to school!

Q: Why would teachers use it?

A: To learn from other teachers and grow! To share the successes schools are having!

Q: Who can see what I post?

A: Anyone. My posts are not private.

Q: What if my students follow me?

A: What am I posting that I wouldn't want them to see? I keep my professional account professional. Students will unfollow me soon enough when they see how boring teachers are. As for Instagram, I post mostly about the children's books I'm reading!

Q: What if parents of my students follow me?

A: Then those parents will be more informed about the teaching world and what I'm considering in the classroom.

Q: What if my administration follows me??!!

A: Same as above. I do not complain on social media, so what does it matter? I feel, as a teacher, I need to be a role model. I wish for my administration to be active on social media as well. Transparency clears up many questions and concerns.

Q: Why would anyone want to see what I post?

A: When I share what we're doing in the classroom, it may inspire others to share as well. When teachers share what they're doing, the community becomes more aware of how school is different from when they were in the system.

Q: How can I get something from using it?

A: Connect with others like you, swap ideas, and soon you'll realize collaboration is at your fingertips.

Consider using a class account. Look through these questions again with this new lens. Having a class account allows you and your students to learn from other classes around the world. Posts are kid-friendly, as most are moderated by the teacher, and they give your students a glimpse into other cultures—clothing, furniture, hairstyles, customs. What a wealth of information your classes can get simply from *lurking*!

Consider the shifts again—with your students in mind. Lurk—and learn about other cultures, customs, and children from around the world. Share some of your students' ideas and connect with other classes in their age group. This may lead to a Skype call or Google Hangout, which is almost like meeting them in person! Parents who follow your class will get a sneak peek into the classroom—as if they were invited in every day. Share your successes, your trials, and your tribulations! After you role model how posts are composed, your students (with you as their guide) can create rules (such as "do not include names," or "remember, our principal will read this") for posting. Once they are aware of the rules and have had some exposure, trust them with the posts. If there is a mistake made, you can always delete something later. Mistakes made from a classroom account can help prevent mistakes when students have their own accounts. At least, that is the goal! For many students, this may be the beginning of their digital footprints. You can help them make it a strong foundation.

There are two difficult obstacles to overcome when you decide to create a class account. Deciding the name is tough. I've seen some that say, for example, @MrsKirrsMinions. I don't want to call my children minions. It's not for me. Some say the room number. I know better than to bet I'll be in the same room for the rest of my years. I settled for @KirrClass. It's not my classROOM, but it is my students who are tweeting (along with me, of course). Plus, it was short, which is always helpful for users who only have 140 characters to spare!

The second hurdle is your willingness to "let go." If you decide to allow students to tweet using the class account, you can overcome this easily by asking them to write it out before they tweet it out. They can show you what they'd like to tweet. In "real life," however, we don't do this. Provide expectations for using the class's Twitter account, and then trust them with their ideas. I have two parameters: Do not include student names, and make sure Mr. Kaye (our principal) or your grandma would be proud of your tweet. If something isn't spelled right, followers will understand it is a child tweeting. You'll either have to get over it, or ask the child to delete it and type it out to tweet once more. Although I am an ELA teacher, I know that the message is more important than the spelling.

> Provide expectations for using the class's Twitter account, and then trust them with their ideas.

In order to collaborate, connect with members of the community using your class account. Let parents and other teachers know what you're doing. Spread the good news! Share your students' smiles! You don't even need to post photos if you feel you have to protect students' anonymity (although the photos and videos help tell more of the story). Your district might already have a hashtag—find out what it is, and use it. If your district or school doesn't yet have one, consider starting one yourself! Share student questions, concerns, and general wonders. Find experts that can help your students with their research. They won't even ask for compensation! You can connect with experts from around the world—seriously. Start the conversations by sharing questions your students ponder. Having students craft the posts makes them more cognizant of spelling, grammar, and the overall message. They have a larger audience for their queries (parents, administration, other classes), so they will work more diligently on getting it "just right." When a student of mine writes a blog post about a favorite book, I tweet out the link. That, in itself, isn't special. What's special is when the author comments on the post, and suddenly the student is having a conversation with the author about decisions she made in her writing! This documented conversation is magic to me and, most importantly, to the child.

Connect your class to authors who use Twitter by finding the author on this helpful document: ***tinyurl.com/AuthorsonTwitter.***

Why are these connections so important? Why are *any* connections vital? Connecting with others gives us a sense of belonging. It also gives us a window into worlds we could not have seen otherwise. It gives your classroom as many experts as you can find! You cannot be the expert in everything you teach. Reach out, and glean from those who want to share their knowledge and passions. Teach students how to learn from others using social media by letting them experiment and by being the role model who uses it appropriately. I tell my students often that the more we learn from others, the more informed our decisions will be. The more we'll see how we are alike, the fewer arguments we'll have. The more we understand one another, the better off we'll be as a society. We will become more empathetic. Use a social media tool to make those crucial connections.

A FLASHBACK

Reading through old blog posts to help me share my message with you, I found this list that I published after just one year of connecting on Twitter:

Since I started creating a PLN (personal learning network) . . .

- I have been challenged.

- I have become more reflective.

- I have been inspired.

- I have had conversations with educators from around the globe.

- I have read more professional literature than ever before.

- I have fallen back in love with photography.

- I found out about free professional development EdCamps and attended on a Saturday in August.

- I began a blog and use it to reflect and share.

- My classroom is transparent.
- My students now have one day a week to learn whatever they want to learn.
- We've Skyped with and learned from four classes this year.
- Participating in the Global Read Aloud, we shared ideas on a Weebly with students from Canada.
- We are a connected classroom, sharing our blog posts through #comments4kids.
- Our classes now have a student station instead of a teacher desk.
- My teaching has transformed … and I hope to keep growing professionally.

FURTHER READING (AND VIEWING!)

» Alyssa Tormala, "Discomfort, Growth, and Innovation" (edutopia.org/blog/ discomfort-growth-and-innovation-alyssa-tormala)

» Sylvia Rosenthal Tolisano, "3 Reasons Why You Should Share and 3 Things You Can Do to Start Sharing" (tinyurl.com/ ShiftShare)

Twitter

» 140 Twitter Tips for Educators (coolcatteacher.com/ 140-twitter-tips-educators/)

» Cybrary Man's (Jerry Blumengarten—@cybraryman1) List of Educational Hashtags (cybraryman.com/edhashtags.html)

» Getting Started on Twitter (cultofpedagogy.com/ twitter-mini-course/)

» Twitter for Educators Course (heinemann.com/products/ DCOCN0014.aspx)

» Twitter—Getting Connected (jcasatodd.com/?page_id=128)

» Twitter Time (for your class account) (kelliholden.wordpress. com/2014/09/08/twitter-time/)

» Twitter Tutorial for Beginners (youtube.com/ watch?v=C69aEmkQp9w)

Instagram

» 10 Surprising Ways to Use Instagram in the Classroom (weareteachers.com/blogs/ post/2014/08/07/10-ways-to-use-instagram-in-the-classroom)

» Instagram in the Gamified Class—Michael Matera (explorelikeapirate.com/instagram-in-the-gamified-class/

» Three Examples of Using Instagram in K-12 Settings—Richard Byrne (freetech4teachers.com/2015/10/three-examples-of-using-instagram-in-k.html)

» Using Instagram for Class—Ashley Callahan (mrscs6thgradelife.blogspot.com/2015/04/using-instagram-for-class.html)

» You're So Vain (or Not So Much)—Erin Olson (rethinkredesign.org/2015/05/20/instagram-youre-so-vain-or-not-so-much/)

Snapchat

» #BookSnaps: Using Snapchat to Create Amazing Reading Reflections (daveburgess.com/booksnaps/)

» 15 Ways to Use Snapchat in Classes and Schools—Matt Miller (ditchthattextbook.com/2016/04/11/15-ways-to-use-snapchat-in-classes-and-schools/)

» The Complete Guide to Snapchat for Teachers and Parents—A.J. Juliani (ajjuliani.com/the-complete-guide-to-snapchat-for-teachers-and-parents/)

» High Schools Experiment with Snapchat to Reach Teens (usnews.com/education/blogs/high-school-notes/2016/03/14/high-schools-experiment-with-snapchat-to-reach-teens)

» Snapchat for Journalists (youtu.be/EUJUP97dKK8)

REFLECTION AND CALL TO ACTION

» Not on social media yet? Try one. Go ahead. Just be yourself on it. Explore. Sit with a child and let him or her show you how to use it.

» Once you're on social media, check out a hashtag. Not new to the tool? Explore a new hashtag, or create one for your school, class, or activity.

» Show your students how to search using a hashtag. (Preview it first, or even take screen shots if you're worried about inappropriate material.) If you find the right one, connect with classes who use this hashtag. This is the safest option—connecting with other classes can open up new worlds for you and your students!

» If you're still on the fence about using one of these tools, ask yourself why. What will you be sharing or possibly seeing? Talk with a friend about their thoughts on these tools. Then talk with more people to hear different perspectives. Set a date a few months from now to once again consider using one of these tools in the future. They change so quickly that maybe they will create new features so you can trust the tool a bit more. Then talk again with peers to hear their thoughts.

_____

_____

_____

_____

9 Student-Directed Learning

Even though I was so many adjectives like scared, sad, confused, tired, and yes, even hungry. I should also be one more adjective. I should be brave.

—*The Meaning of Maggie* by Megan Jean Sovern

"Can I learn more magic tricks today, since I don't have my other materials?"

"Can I get my phone so I can download my videos?"

"Can we work together? We both have DIY projects, but different materials."

"Can you mail this for me?"

"Can I work on this at home?"

"Can my dad help me?"

"Can I change my topic?"

My answer to all of these ... "Why not?" followed up at times with "What issues could arise that we can prepare for?"

Who is my inspiration for teaching? The kids. My answer will always be the kids. Their questions keep me on my toes, and they keep me inspired. I'll be the first to admit it, however—I am *still* too much the "teacher" in the room. I am still working on creating a culture that makes students the experts. I want them to ask questions like those above to one another so they don't have to come to me so often. Maybe it's because I still want to have a handle on what's going on in the classroom, or maybe it's a result of all the years prior when the teacher was the "end-all be-all" of final decisions. Still, I find answering with "Why not?" makes things easier on them and even easier on me. If what they are doing is safe and respectful, I'm probably going to be okay with it, especially during student-directed learning.

Before I incorporated Genius Hour into our days, I was fortunate enough to attend a workshop by Ewan McIntosh (@ewanmcintosh), regarding design thinking. The question we worked on most of the day was this: What are some problems at your school? Which of these problems do you feel you can help with? Let's start working on solving it *today.*

My own personal questions stemmed from a brainstorming activity about the problems at my school. I wondered, *How can I get my kids reading more than one book a quarter? How can I have the kids do more work than me?* (We were working much harder on the rubrics than the students were working on their projects to show they were reading!) And this is how my first version of what is now called "Genius Hour" began in my seventh grade ELA classroom.

This type of learning was the catalyst for all the other shifts in this book. This was the largest shift in my career, I believe, because it made me question so much more of what was happening in classrooms. It brought student ideas and skills to the forefront. I learned to *trust* the children. This is why I was able to shift aspects of the classroom itself, discussions, homework, and even grading. My students from four years ago would not recognize my teaching style should they visit today. The biggest result of including Genius Hour in my pedagogy is that I am now comfortable enough to offer more student voice and choice in *all* we do.

> ## The biggest result of including Genius Hour in my pedagogy is that I am now comfortable enough to offer more student voice and choice in *all* we do.

This chapter focuses on how you can slowly let go of monopolizing students' time in school. My dream is to instill in all students a love of learning, providing them time in the classroom to learn what they want to learn—not just what *I* deem important. We'll focus on what this time is, why it's crucial we try some aspect of it in our schools, and then what it includes. I will not go into step-by-step directions on how to incorporate this time. You'll find various ways on how to implement something like Genius Hour included under the Further Reading section at the end of this chapter. Before we begin, here are a few more questions that popped up for me to consider as I learned more about student-centered learning:

» Do I model my own self-directed learning with my students?

» How can I make learning more relevant for my students?

» How do I show respect for the naturally curious learners in my charge?

GENIUS HOUR—THE NAME

The name itself has gotten a lot of backlash, and I have even changed the name in my own class. There are so many names teachers have chosen for this time. (See many names for student-directed learning here: tinyurl.com/NamesForGH.) The name you choose may not be popular with some teachers or students, but you have to choose what works for you and your students. Include them in the decision! What name would reflect what you want from this time? Aside from names, the biggest negative I've heard about the *concept* is that it is not 100 percent of our teaching time. What an intriguing concept to consider! There are some teachers—and entire schools—who are working towards this goal of student-directed learning 100 percent of the time. However, I would be remiss if I didn't share with you the arguments against this type of learning, such as "liking doesn't correlate with more learning" or "there is no research that says it works." Head to the pink tabs on this link to dip your toes into the opposition: tinyurl.com/ShiftOpposingViews. Reading these has given me solid counter arguments to consider, and I have often tweaked our plans as a result. (Be sure to welcome opposing views—use them to help you reflect more and work better towards what's right in your classroom.)

Throughout this chapter, I'll refer to this student-directed learning as Genius Hour. This dedicated time will be what you feel you can provide—thirty minutes, forty-five minutes, one hour, or more. Whatever you choose, your students will benefit from this time. Should you choose to take this on, you need to call it something based on what you believe it will become. P.E. teachers—consider "Coach Your Class" (see the story here: tinyurl.com/ShiftCoach). Art teachers—how about "Da Vinci Day" (tinyurl.com/ShiftDavinciDay)? As long as you have a name for it, it will grow and branch out into many aspects of your school day. Genius Hour—even before it had a name in my classroom—has sprung many small shifts that have led to the best years of my teaching career so far.

As I write this chapter, I need to let you know that I no longer conduct "Genius Hour" in room 239. I have relocated our time spent on student-driven learning and creating to the end of each quarter, so that my students and I have the time to conduct one-on-one conferences about their learning (and decide a final grade). We now call this time "Independent Inquiry," and it mostly resembles "Innovation Weeks" that are popular among some teaching circles. It's still Genius Hour; it's just packaged differently. I had to make the change so that this time spent with students is available to me at the *end* of each quarter, and not spread throughout. As I'll continue to share in my workshops and presentations, whatever you do has to work for *you*. If you are not comfortable with something, the students won't get out of it what you hope for them. The focus in our classroom is still on student curiosity. Their ideas will be honored and celebrated, and they will still be practicing the habits of lifelong learners. This adjustment of timing works for me, and I can still be a "Genius Hour Evangelist"! In the meantime, my students are directing more of their own learning throughout the year than ever before in my career.

WHAT IS GENIUS HOUR?

Genius Hour is authentic, student-driven, and inquiry-driven. We ask questions, and try to find answers. It is giving students ample time to be creative. Genius Hour helps cultivate lifelong learners. Questions can come from interests. Interests can lead to passions. Passions can then lead to purpose. ← This is my goal as an educator. It's tough when I see seventh graders wrapped up in me, me, me, me. I'd really love to see them invested in helping others. It takes a lot of time, patience, caring, and guidance in order for some children to get to this point. I won't let that stop me from trying!

Teachers who have delved into Genius Hour know that one hour is not enough. However, this dedicated time (no matter how long) is for students to take control of their own learning. It is a time for students to find out or learn more about what they love—and to learn about how to get closer to solving problems that break their hearts. When something about our teaching doesn't feel right, we look for answers. We give ourselves time to work on what's bothering us—in teaching and outside of school. When do our students get this time during school? Consider what could happen if students began finding and then trying to solve problems! Genius Hour has the possibility to impact our own students' lives, as well as the lives of many others.

Clearly, I love this time for self-directed, exploratory learning. And I'm not alone. Take a look at how a few of my students define Genius Hour:

> ## "Genius Hour is where you get to pick whatever project you want to do, and you get to explore it further."
>
> —Sarah C.

Sarah's Genius Hour time was spent finding ways to help animals at no-kill shelters. Her box for donated newspapers had a permanent place in our room the rest of the year.

> ## "It's a chance for us to change something in the world."
>
> —Erin R.

Erin was finding out a way for our students to be allowed to chew gum in classes. She connected with classroom Twitter accounts to do some of her research.

> ## "Genius Hour is when kids get to express themselves once a week by doing what they love."
>
> —Jenna M.

Jenna spent Genius Hour time on her own projects (from writing "how to" blog posts to DIY projects) and helping others on theirs.

> # "Genius Hour is a time where you have the choice to change something, whether it's the way you think, or maybe it could even change the world."
>
> —Ashly Z.

Ashly read during class. At home, she taught her "old dog" new tricks. (And, yes, her mom brought her dog to school for her presentation! We took the kids outside for that one.)

SHIFT "PBL"

There are currently at least three different ways to define PBL:

Project-Based Learning

According to the Buck Institute for Education, project-based learning "is a teaching method in which students gain knowledge and skills by working for an extended period of time to investigate and respond to a complex question, problem, or challenge" (bie.org).

The essential elements are much the same as in Genius Hour. According to the BIE website, the project is based on teaching students skills and building twenty-first-century competencies, "such as problem solving, critical thinking, collaboration, communication, and creativity/innovation." Students are involved in in-depth inquiry, based on a driving question. Another goal of project-based learning is for students to present their work to a public audience.

Project-based learning is a large step toward Genius Hour. Students still have choice in some aspects of this type of learning, but it is the *teacher* who generates the question. This is not yet student-driven learning.

Problem-Based Learning

Problem-based learning includes the same essential elements as project-based learning. The question to ask next is—WHO is finding the problem? This has the potential to be student-driven learning—if it's not the teachers, but the *students* finding the problem.

Passion-Based Learning

Passion-based learning can also be Genius Hour. If it is truly passion-based learning, it will be lifelong learning as well. Students who are acting on their own particular passions are sure to continue and evolve this "project" for years to come. Angela Maiers is my top motivator and role model for encouraging passion-based learning. She stresses the importance of not only asking what students love, but also what breaks their hearts. She knows that a passion is something you *must* do—something that, no matter the obstacles or the pain that comes with it, you will *continue* doing. It's part of you. If you and your students are fortunate enough to be able to spend the time and tap into their passions, you will have success at implementing Genius Hour (or whatever you want to call your student-driven learning). Depending on what ages your students are, you may find this type of learning to be just beyond your reach with some of your students. Many of my seventh graders have not had opportunities in school to share their passions. The majority of them do not seem to know (or be able to recognize) what their passions are. This is all the more reason to start something like Genius Hour in your classroom—at any age.

MORE ON "PBL"

Each of these is a scaffold in itself. Consider the shifts they include. First, the teacher comes up with a project, and students complete it with the teacher's parameters (including rubrics) in mind. This could be your first step towards letting students work on a larger project they choose. Perhaps you have topics that you'll be covering in your curriculum each semester, and you allow students the choice of which to study. Second, the teacher shares problems (from the curriculum) with students, and they solve it within the teacher's parameters. Perhaps the teacher opens it up so students can choose how they'd like to share their learning. Third, the students themselves come up with the problem. The teacher may or may not include parameters. Fourth, we ask students to use their passions to direct their learning. Much of this type of learning is wide open. The lack of guardrails can seem overwhelming for students who are used to teacher parameters. Consider scaffolding for students who take a while figuring out what to do. Some students will be ready to fly as soon as you describe your goals; others will need you to give them parameters. Don't be afraid to keep options wide open, and then scaffold for those students who could use a hand. You are still the teacher! Your guidance is expected and valued. Students' reactions will alert you to which students need more guidance, and which you can let work on their own for some time.

WHY? WHAT'S THE POINT OF STUDENT-DIRECTED LEARNING?

Why hand over precious time to the students? We must always go back to the question of *why*. At some point, you may be asked to prove to parents and administration why this time is so valuable. If you don't understand the reasons for it, why should others buy in to it? I'd like to help you understand why it's so worthwhile.

Have you ever said something like this?

"I teach preschool, and we are only in school for half the day."

"Students can learn what they want to learn when they go home."

"When we have indoor recess, isn't that like Genius Hour?"

"I only have my U.S. History class for 250 minutes a week."

Time is precious to us all—no matter what age we teach, no matter what subject. Is time also precious to our students? Glimpses into students' lives show that time is indeed precious:

"I've got basketball practice all week, and then we have our tournament on the weekend!"

"After dance this week, my mom and I are visiting my grandma and helping her move."

"We have a test in social studies tomorrow and I have my C.E.R. due in science!"

"I don't know if I'll have time to read this weekend, because we're going on a twelve-mile hike for scouts!"

For us to even consider "giving up" time each week, we must look at why this time would be beneficial to our students.

Engagement and motivation are at an all-time low.

Our students are constantly learning more outside of school than we were ever able to learn. They have computers in their pockets that can answer questions in a matter of seconds. It's a hundred times easier for students to find information now than it was when I was in school. When students put their phones in their lockers for the day and are asked to learn what we tell them they must learn, engagement immediately drops, no matter how good a teacher we think we are. After we cut off this extra arm they've grown so used to having attached to them, we then expect them to be able to concentrate on what we have to say. We expect them to become interested in the information we are so passionately sharing with them. We've got curriculum to teach, and we're going to do our best to make sure they learn it, even if we have to stand on our heads to help them focus!

The fact is, in our students' minds, it's all about them. If you're teaching science, and you've got a student who loves science, that student will most likely be engaged in your curriculum—and the extent could be dependent on how passionate the teacher may seem. In the next school hour, this student could be asked to learn about something he or she is totally *not* into. The motivation to learn is suddenly absent, and it has nothing to do with how passionate that teacher may or may not be. Take out the teacher altogether, and you can still have a student who is disengaged with the curriculum. I am hearing more and more from teachers and parents that "(Insert name here) will put forth the effort if it is important enough to him." How do we make our subject relevant to students who are "just not interested"? How do we make our curriculum more accessible and relevant for every child who is used to having information at their fingertips?

We need to focus on teaching the *child* and not solely focus on our curriculum. What can we do to engage our students in our curriculum, even if it's not something they're normally interested in? Personal projects are where students have ownership over what they are learning. They are our key to accessing more about students' interests, strengths, and struggles. Using this information will help us connect our curriculum to all of our students, regardless of where their interests lie.

While you are learning about the children, the children will be immersed in learning something they want to learn, and you'll see their skills shine. You'll also have the time to sit with them and talk with them about something they love. You'll be able to use these conversations and observations to better teach your "normal" curriculum and make it more relevant to each student. What better feedback to help you tailor future lessons to your students!

Creativity has declined.

It seems as if every year there is something new that teachers must do. Whether it relates to state standards and testing, or new administration in our district, teachers have a lot to implement in their classrooms. The first thing to go is usually creativity. Don't get me wrong, teachers are trying to be creative in giving options to their students, but students themselves don't get much time to show their creativity in classes. Sir Ken Robinson's famous TED talk "Do Schools Kill Creativity?" explains just what schools are doing, and gives us plenty of reasons to incorporate student-driven learning. He gives evidence that shows we squander children's tremendous talents—"pretty ruthlessly." He says we get "educated out of creativity" when we attend school and warns us that teachers are grooming students to be university professors; that's not what we'll need in the near future. Our goal should no longer be to produce students who have academic ability—the goals of our system need to be changed. His main point in the TED talk is that "creativity now is as important in education as literacy, and we should treat it with the same status."

There is no room for failure.

In order to prepare our students for the future, we need to give them opportunities to create—and risk failure. Sir Ken Robinson also reminds us that kids will take a chance. "If they don't know, they'll have a go." They're not frightened to be wrong. Once a grade is attached, the fear of failure is so strong that many students will only take the safe route and not try something new. They won't push themselves. They'll only do what we ask of them, and nothing more! Future careers require creativity and entrepreneurship. When do we give students work that is free from risks? If we are not giving that time to students, they will not be ready for those careers (we can't even imagine) that are coming down the pike.

We need problem finders.

Ewan McIntosh speaks of the need for "problem finders" in his TEDxLondon Talk, "What's next?" We want "young people that can go out into the world and find problems that really need solving and have the capacity to go and start solving them with their peers." We have enough time in our content when we give "pseudo problems" to students during our week. Generations have been brought up to believe that teachers give the problems, and students solve them. We often give students "stupid problems that don't matter." When do students get to find problems that matter to **them**? When do they then get a chance to start solving these problems? When do they get to feel as if they're doing something *worthwhile*?

Students don't have opportunities in school to make their own decisions.

You know it's true. We expect students to ask us if they need to use the bathroom, for goodness' sake. Yet in the next minute, we expect them to be able to "act their age." We expect them to be mature enough to make certain decisions, and yet we do not offer them enough opportunities to practice this decision-making. It often seems as if everything we give them is a final assessment instead of practice.

We need to cultivate lifelong learners.

The more material and curriculum we give students to learn, the less inquisitive they become and the more apt they are to be complacent and passive instead. They get used to others telling them what to learn. This won't fly once they get out of school. We need to make school a place that represents authentic learning. When do you learn something new? When it's something *you* want to learn. Let's start making school more authentic by giving students time to learn what *they* want to learn. What do they really need to learn? They need to learn *how* to learn. They can't do this if we dictate the learning every minute.

WHAT DOES STUDENT-DIRECTED LEARNING INCLUDE?

Inquiry—Students ask questions that cannot be answered by a simple search or two. These questions range from "Can I learn how to play a song on the ukulele?" to "Which cancer should doctors learn how to cure first?" Some ideas begin with "What would happen if _____?" while others are not questions, and can begin with "I'm going to learn how to _____." Whatever ideas your students come up with, they are generated by the students and not by the teacher. Ignite their curiosity, and you foster their love of learning.

> Check out a few Genius Hour ideas from students around the world on this document:
> **tinyurl.com/GHExamples.**

Creativity

Creativity is required throughout this learning process, especially when problems arise. Some characteristics that come along with creativity are perseverance, courage, adaptability, and stamina. Since the teacher is only the facilitator, students are encouraged to find solutions to problems on their own or with help from friends or experts. Their persistence and creativity is tested again and again.

Planning

You've heard it said (and perhaps said it yourself) that students don't know how to plan when it comes to long-term projects. Genius Hour gives students plenty of practice doing just that! You may find yourself scaffolding some directions or asking some students to fill in a calendar for plans, but the workload and implementation is ultimately up to them. You may have a handful of students who "don't know what to do" during this time. This is most likely because they've never been asked to learn for themselves in school. This is also justification to try student-directed learning in your class!

Purpose or Product

If you haven't yet tried this in your class, you might think the *product* is where the magic happens, but truly the magic is all throughout the *process* students go through during student-driven learning. However, the question I hear most often is this: "What is the best project your students have done?"

What they're looking for is a project that will make the world a better place. The fact is, your class might not come up with a project that will make others' lives better. They will, however, come up with a project that is purposeful to them, if no one else. Our dream is that they will find a passion and be able to change the world a tiny bit at a time with their work, but the reality is that we are dealing with children who often only think of themselves. You have to be okay with this, or you won't want to continue. We have to start somewhere. Since one of the major goals of student-driven learning is student engagement, what better way to engage students than to let them figure out what they love and let them head down that path? Then consider the research skills and the habits of perseverance they will develop while following their own interests! If you are requiring your students to make a difference during this time, you should get them involved in *Choose2Matter*, and let Angela Maiers light a fire under them to make a difference for someone else.

Sharing

When are students asked to share? When do they get a chance to talk with their friends about what they're doing, what they love, or what bothers them? In our middle school setting, they may be able to do so during lunch, but that's about it. From bell to bell, teachers are asking students to pay attention to their content, and not bring outside issues in. At this point in a child's life, when her body is going through tons of changes and he needs to feel accepted the most, we often skip any sharing. "Let's get to work!" when that bell rings and keep them until the next bell, focusing on what we need to cover. Student-driven learning includes, at the very least, weekly sharing of ideas, likes and dislikes, troubles and successes. Being able to share what they love builds more of that culture of collaboration and inquiry. If we want students to be inquisitive and collaborative, we need to give them time—on something in which they are personally invested. This helps students feel like they matter, offers other students a time and place to give assistance, and it helps students develop further trust in their teacher as well.

Reflection (and wish for lifelong learning)

Reflection helps students recognize what they're doing well, and what they could be doing better. Give them an outlet to reflect on and then share with others their struggles and successes. Always ask, "How could you have done better?" Teachers have a hard enough time finding the minutes for much-needed reflection. Some reflections are simply two to five minutes. Denise Krebs has a great reflection (using a scale) on the Genius Hour wiki listed in the Further Reading section of this chapter. You can also use sticky notes, Google forms, or even a quick overall "thumbs up, middle, or down" at the end of a session. We need to help students build this skill so that it becomes commonplace for them as they grow.

Student-driven learning is the perfect time for reflection and dialogue. Reflection is where the deeper learning takes place. Some (many?) projects won't live up to your expectations. (Example: Frozen Marbles? Really?? Yes: tinyurl.com/ShiftFrozenMarbles) No one is to say whether the students' projects are valuable except the student, and yet teachers will observe some students "wasting their time." As my husband reminds me, "They don't know what they want to learn." Reflection, then, is where you'll see the value. After all, the journey *is* more important than the destination. If students learn from the process by reflecting on how they could improve the next time, the journey alone was worth it. When you run into students who do not respond to this type of learning, remember that no one system or idea is perfect for every student. And, of course, not every child will know how to be honest in their reflection. We need to provide the time for them to practice this valuable skill.

> Need further encouragement for how to cope with and help students who seem unmotivated? Read my blog post about what's caused me to question the value of Genius Hour: **tinyurl.com/ShiftNotPerfect.**

WHAT'S IN IT FOR ME?

It makes me sad that teachers may still be asking this question, even after understanding the many reasons *why* we need to incorporate Genius Hour into our classes. It's all about the students, and what's in it for them. Yet we know teachers still wonder "What's in it for me?" because we are all under stress to teach certain curriculum within a certain number of days. What are you currently teaching? What do you consider more important to teach? Is it the content? Or is it the *students*? Either way, providing time throughout your year for this type of learning will help you teach both—your content *and* your students.

How will implementing dedicated time to student choice help you teach both your content and your students? Consider this: How do you build trust with students? You connect with them. You learn more about them. You talk with them—about topics other than school. During this time, your job is to do just that. Do not look through your email. Do not work on your own project (do this at home). Do not do other work. Spend this time speaking one-on-one with students about their passions, their struggles, their talents, their workload at home, etc. Make a checklist of some sort so you can keep track of who you talked with each session. The next session, talk with the students you missed. Keeping track keeps you accountable to check in with each student on a regular basis. During these conferences, you'll start by asking about their projects. By showing students that you value this time, you'll find out more than you ever thought possible. You'll learn what makes them tick. You'll learn what type of learners they are. You will learn what they are skilled at and what they wish they knew. You'll learn about their strengths and struggles, and be able to apply these to your lessons. **All of your lessons will revolve around your students' skills and needs.** Your curriculum will still be covered because your students will be more engaged in your lessons. They will trust you more and, as a result, they'll pay more attention. Again, all of your lessons will revolve around your students' skills and needs. And isn't this the ultimate goal? Providing time such as Genius Hour impacts the way your students learn—in school and out.

Consider more questions: Who is in charge of learning in your classroom? Who does the most work in your classroom? Who does the creating, constructing, producing, and performing? The answer must be the learners. Make sure everyone in the classroom is learning—by doing.

One way #GeniusHour affects the rest of your week...

All of your lessons will revolve around your students' skills and needs.

@JoyKirr

SERIOUSLY... WHAT DO I HAVE TO DO IN ORDER TO MAKE THIS HAPPEN?

You could just jump in. That's what I did. I realized that I needed students driving more of the learning than I was allowing, and I carved out an hour of our week—every week—so this could happen. If you'd like to jump in tomorrow, ask your students, "What would you like to learn?" or "What problem would you like to solve?" or "What is your passion?" or all of these. If you are not quite there—yet—you can begin by making small shifts ...

Many of us are content-area specialists. I have my reading specialist degree and feel as if I'm still a specialist in teaching students who are deaf and hard of hearing. Some teachers are specialists in biology, the Civil War, Motown music, Leonardo da Vinci, and yet, we should *all* be "student specialists." Where do we get that degree? In the countless one-on-one conversations we should be having with students each hour. This is never-ending professional development. It is continuing education that we must attend.

Once you are fully invested in dedicating time to allow students to personalize their own learning, you may find that you don't need any type of name for it. It might begin to come naturally. I've noticed this past year that, even if we didn't have our "Independent Inquiry" weeks, my students still own a lot more of their learning than in previous years in our room. There are many instances where choices they make become a guide to what they will learn. I'm slowly working towards a goal of incorporating student-directed learning into *all* we do in our ELA classroom.

HOW DO I BEGIN?

There are many ways to begin. Heck, there are books on how to go about this type of learning in the classroom! See the list under Further Reading. What is important to know is that you do not have to have perfect plans in order to begin. You do not need to be an expert. Just get started. Ask the question, "What do you want to learn/create/do?" Then let the learning happen from there. All of my resources are on the Genius Hour/20 percent Time LiveBinder (tinyurl com/GHLiveBinder). Take the time to browse. You'll learn from thousands of teachers who have shared resources with the world. It's difficult at the beginning, but when you see students' growth in their progress and their reflections, it's truly rewarding.

> When you check out the LiveBinder, it may appear overwhelming because it's constantly evolving. Check out **tinyurl.com/ShiftBinderHelp** for help navigating this behemoth!

FURTHER READING

» Angela Maiers and Amy Sandvold, *The Passion-driven Classroom: A Framework for Teaching and Learning* (Eye on Education: 2010)

» Angela Maiers' Choose2Matter initiative: choose2matter. org and ebook *Liberating Genius*: choose2matter.org/ liberatinggenius/

» Buck Institute for Education, "What is Project-Based Learning?" (bie.org/about/what_pbl)

» Denise Krebs and Gallit Zvi, *The Genius Hour Guidebook: Fostering Passion, Wonder, and Inquiry in the Classroom* (Routledge: 2016)

» Don Wettrick, *Pure Genius: Building a Culture of Innovation and Taking 20 Percent Time to the Next Level* (Dave Burgess Consulting, 2014)

» Ewan McIntosh, TEDx London: "What's Next?" (youtu.be/JUnhyyw8_kY)

» Genius Hour / 20 percent Time LiveBinder: tinyurl.com/GHLiveBinder

» Genius Hour Wiki (includes chat archives): geniushour.wikispaces.com/

» Kevin Brookhouser, *The 20time Project: How Educators Can Launch Google's Formula for Future-Ready Innovation* (20time.org: 2015)

» Sir Ken Robinson, "Do Schools Kill Creativity?" (ted.com/ talks/ken_robinson_says_schools_kill_creativity?language=en)

REFLECTION AND CALL TO ACTION

» Reflect on where you already give students choice. Where are your gaps?

» If you're not ready to jump in with both feet, find places in your curriculum where students can choose what to learn. Ask them for help designing "me time" if you need it.

» Are you on Twitter? Look through the #geniushour and #20time hashtags. Join a chat! Ask questions! Learn from others around the world who are giving their students time to learn what THEY want to learn—in class.

» Look for a kindred spirit at your school or district. Share your ideas, and see who'll collaborate with you on your ideas. It's difficult to go it alone, or to be the first. It's easier if you have a partner!

» Look through the LiveBinder (tinyurl.com/GHLiveBinder). If you are still not convinced, start with the "WHY" tab. If you want to get started right away, head to the "How to Get Started" tab or to the grade-level tab that works for you under "Grade-Level Stories."

» Consider a name for personalized learning that can work for you in your situation. On the LiveBinder, check out the tab under "How to Get Started" titled "Names/Ideas" for suggestions.

_____

_____

10 Resistance

Dare to poke your head up, dare to stand out from the crowd, and you risk being gobbled up.

—*Hour of the Bees* by Lindsay Eagar

We need to be challenged in order to learn.

—*Because of Mr. Terupt* by Rob Buyea

In for a "routine procedure" at the doctor's office after work, the machine breaks, and technician Anne-Marie has to reset it. This leaves time for conversation, and she finds out I'm a teacher. I let her know that seventh grade is the best grade—they're still innocent, they don't cry (much), I don't have to tie their shoes, the things that come out of their mouths are hilarious...

"So do you give homework?"

I chuckle, not knowing how to respond. So I ask, "Where does this question come from?"

"My son goes to Bartlett High School, and they're suddenly not giving any homework, giving 4s, 3s, 2s, and 1s, and they can turn in all of their work as late as they want, as long as they get it in before the semester is over. It's crazy."

My brain is going in twenty different directions. So I do what I learned from a workshop with Rick Wormeli: ask a question. "What do you think the 4s, 3s, 2s, and 1s represent?"

"Oh, I know they're grades. It's just like A through D, but my son should NOT be getting a 'satisfactory' or a '2' just for trying. That doesn't happen when he gets to college. You don't get a grade for trying."

"If a '4' equals an 'A' and a '2' equals a 'C' in your eyes, then isn't that what he's getting for working on that standard? Do you think he is doing 'satisfactory' work?"

Dodging the real question, she responds, "All I know is, the colleges are going to have deadlines and not give credit for him trying."

I sigh. "I think if the high school communicated with you more before they began, you might see some value in what they're doing."

"Oh, they've sent me email after email, and letters home, but I don't have time to read it all. I have three jobs, put three of my four children through college with my own cash, and now this last one is going to just fall on his butt because he doesn't have to do anything to get through high school."

I don't know what I say at this point, but I know what I think: Isn't having your work in by the end of the semester a deadline? When did being 'satisfactory' not count? She would loathe what I'm doing in our class.

She continues, "High school is supposed to get kids ready for college. That's its purpose."

"So here's a question for you—What's the purpose of middle school?"

"To get kids ready for high school, of course, and elementary school is supposed to get kids ready for middle school, and life, really. It's all supposed to get them ready for life.

Teach them responsibility and deadlines. Even if you don't want a real job, but you want to work at the mall, they'll fire you if you're late even two times. But now my son can turn in anything as late as he wants and he's not learning a thing about the real world."

At some point, she comes back to her original question: "Do you give homework?"

"I give regular homework of reading at least twenty minutes a night, and the students set goals every two weeks. They reflect every two weeks on their goal of how well they did on reading for twenty minutes a night on average."

"Tell me to read, and that's torturing me. The only reading I do is in line at the grocery store."

The cold, hard truth is that we have some parents like this. Oh, shucks. We might as well go a bit further—we have some teachers like this. Confession: I was one of them (except for the whole "reading is torture" bit). How can we expect parents—or teachers—to know why we're changing education if they don't want any change? Why should they want change when they themselves "turned out okay" under the current system? And why should they want to change when they haven't been allowed time to find out the reasons why certain changes can benefit our students?

Before you try to tackle resistance, try answering the following questions for each of the shifts you've decided to implement:

» Is the shift you've made purposeful?

» Have you defined that purpose?

» Why did you make this shift?

» What are your goals?

» How is this shift learner-centered?

» How is it personalized?

» How did this shift affect your students?

» What other effects have you observed?

This chapter is about resistance. Obstacles. People and things that will try to stop you from the smallest of shifts in your classroom. I've shared with you how my thinking shifted after I began changing the culture in my own classroom. I'm so far removed from where I was just eight years ago, as a result of (another confession coming) a slow-as-molasses mind shift. Here are the steps you'll find you go through. The challenge is to see if you can skip a few and just jump to the mindset of "I don't care what y'all think. This is my career, I'm a professional, and I'm doing what I believe is best for children!"

STEP 1: DENIAL

Shut the door. Don't let your administration know what you're doing, let alone the teacher down the hall. Heaven forbid they walk by at the "wrong" time! You're giving kids time to read independently in class? *What*?!? That's not "teaching"! Student laughter is leaking out into the hallway or maybe you have twenty students talking at once, and no one can find you because you look like one of the kids? You wonder aloud, "Who's in control of this class?!" Just shut the door. You are afraid of being judged and are not ready to hear criticism. You're still in the experimental stage and need to see if your hypotheses will work. You need to refocus on the reasons why you are doing these things in your class before you are ready to defend your actions to nay-sayers. What would you say to a coworker or administrator who might question your lessons?

STEP 2: INQUIRE

Ask a close friend, mentor, or your evaluator about the ideas you're trying out in the classroom. Ask him or her to help you further your dream of what you think is right for students. You'd be surprised all you can glean from asking for help. Most people *want* to help—it's human nature. My parents taught me that. After one observation by my assistant principal, I shared a concern I had about a student with her at our follow-up meeting. She simply asked, "What are you planning to do about it next?" I use this question often now whenever I have something I want resolved. She did not give me an answer. Again and again, the questions themselves are what drive us to action. Keep asking the questions so you can reflect on your own practice. I do not have it all together. I reflect on my own work and ask for help—often.

STEP 3: SHARE SOME IDEAS ...
ON SOCIAL MEDIA.

I shared "crazy" ideas on Twitter before I ever shared at my own school. The community I had *hand-picked* to follow and converse with was very supportive and encouraging. If they weren't, I'd simply stop looking at their tweets. This is one of the benefits of building a professional learning network on Twitter, Instagram, Facebook, Voxer, Snapchat and any other up-and-coming modes of social media. You choose the people in your "tribe." You create your own professional development. Teachers on Twitter are my go-to when I have a question, and they're often the first people I share great ideas with. Ideas that are beneficial for students spread like wildfire, and then passionate teachers *add on* to these ideas and share them back with you to make them *even better*. I have always been fortunate to have supportive teaching partners as well. The teachers I'm connected with have a growth mindset and want to become better teachers so their students thrive. While online, I surround myself with them so I can continue to keep my mind open and ready to learn more from others. I am also connected to teachers who make it their responsibility to challenge other teachers' ideas. When others question my ideas (again with the all-important questions!), it forces me to go back to the reasons why and helps me make my argument stronger—or I may just need to adjust my thinking.

STEP 4: SHARE SOME IDEAS ... WITH PARENTS.

You can begin with a "Welcome to __ grade/subject" letter or video sent home at the beginning of the school year. Let them know that things will be a bit different in your class this year, as you're trying to always improve in the best interest of children. This should be welcomed, as variety in teaching styles is valuable. Maybe you're a fan of the newsletter or blog post once a month. Communicating with parents is a crucial step towards getting students, other teachers, and your administration to buy into all the shifting you're doing in class. Let parents know the purpose behind the shifts before they even *think* to challenge you.

STEP 5: SHARE SOME IDEAS ... WITH YOUR COWORKERS.

I saved this for step five, because I don't like being shot down, and this is the route I took myself. I have often thought teachers at my own school are my harshest critics. I've realized, however, that many times it's only in my own mind. Why is this? I believe it's because I'm afraid of failure, and I'm taking many risks. I am still unsure of what I'm doing in the classroom. I have realized as well that I react—instead of stopping to listen and trying to recognize other teachers' perspectives. It is my own fault that I do not take the time to explain the reasons behind my actions to teachers at my own school. I am a people-pleaser. This behavior, however, can be a detriment to yourself and also to your students. Since we see one another every day, coworkers are like family.

Some days are easier than others, and we'll be with them through better or worse; the workload, our students, our families at home, and our health contribute to our dispositions on any particular day. Hence, the reason I'm hesitant to cause waves. Sharing ideas with my coworkers has been my last step in shifting my classroom. Resistance, however, can happen anywhere, at any time—especially if you're trying things that are different from the norm.

→ RESISTANCE ←

It's inevitable. It can happen at any one of these steps, and will probably happen at *each* one.

What's the solution?

→ COMMUNICATION ←

SHIFT THIS!

RESISTANCE

SHARE.

KEEP THE CONVERSATION GOING.

ASK MORE QUESTIONS!

COMMUNICATE WITH ADMINISTRATION

There is the phrase out in the teaching world: "It's easier to ask for forgiveness instead of permission." It basically means do what you've got to do, and then ask if it's okay that you did it. The people-pleaser in me will have none of that. Go in and talk to your administration face to face. Have the research with you for support. The first time I shared a shift I'd already begun with my former principal, I was very open to any answer he might give. I explained what I was trying, then asked, "Do you think what I'm doing is right for the students?"

He simply replied, "Do *you* believe it is?"

That's all it took. It was yet another question I could apply to everything I was doing.

Is what I am doing *right for students?*

It was my own question, and yet I now knew I had to believe it in my heart in order to continue. You have to believe it is right for students in order for it to work in the first place, and you need to believe it is right for students in order to share with others and convince them of the many benefits for children.

I now have a sign on my door—for administration, other teachers, and parents alike. Heck, sometimes even the *students* read it! ;)

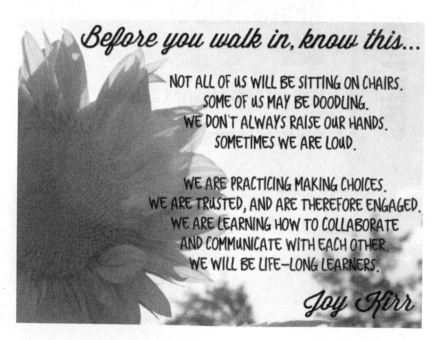

Before you walk in, know this...

NOT ALL OF US WILL BE SITTING ON CHAIRS.
SOME OF US MAY BE DOODLING.
WE DON'T ALWAYS RAISE OUR HANDS.
SOMETIMES WE ARE LOUD.

WE ARE PRACTICING MAKING CHOICES.
WE ARE TRUSTED, AND ARE THEREFORE ENGAGED.
WE ARE LEARNING HOW TO COLLABORATE
AND COMMUNICATE WITH EACH OTHER.
WE WILL BE LIFE-LONG LEARNERS.

Joy Kirr

I had originally posted this as a blog post (tinyurl.com/ShiftDisclaimer), calling it a "disclaimer." My associate principal at the time called it an "advertisement." What an affirmation! I believe in it, so I display it proudly and explain it to anyone who shows interest.

COMMUNICATE WITH PARENTS

Recognize that the factory model of school has been around for generations. The parents went through this model, and it "worked for me"! After all, didn't it work for you? Ignoring all the other factors that join forces in educating children (parents, atmosphere, wealth, travels, opportunities, etc.), the public school building is still how parents remember it. The teacher directs, and the students comply, like a shepherd and his flock—no veering from the plan. There's no time! The little ones have to learn to write (many of them now head to school already knowing how to read). The bells ring in a middle or high school, and the students move through the herd for four minutes just to sit once again. Unless parents are in your classroom many times during the year, they really have **no clue** what's going on. If they hear something from their child and repeat it back to you (all askew of what you were really doing that day), you could say, "I won't believe what they say about you if you don't believe what they say about me."

At any rate, you need to inform them—multiple times—of the reasons behind what you're doing. Then they won't need to rely on their child for the information. Yes, you're "putting yourself out there" by trying new things. So provide the reasons why. How can you do this, if parents might not even read your emails? Share what you can, in as many places as you can, as often as you can. It will cut down the number of parents who question your reasons for trying different things in your classroom, and it may even make them excited that their child has you for a teacher!

Put all your information in one central location.

Our class website for parents and students (and now teachers too) mentioned in Chapter Four is used as a central location for my beliefs, our curriculum, and our procedures. Embed what you learn and what you want to share in this one central location. Each time you send an email, a tweet, or other post, include or embed the link to this central location, so it becomes familiar to parents. Your website doesn't have to be completed all in one month. You can start small and add to it once you see how you'd like to organize it. I checked out many other teachers' websites before I settled on a platform, and after three years with it, I'm finally happy with the format. Adding to it (and taking off old material) is an ever-evolving process.

Take your time during Parent Night.

Share your beliefs with parents when you meet them as a group for Open House, Meet the Teacher Night, or another time you set up just for this purpose. We have eight minutes per class period for this night (I get sixteen, as I have students for two periods). If you have elementary students, you've (hopefully) got a nice chunk of time. You don't need to worry about sharing curriculum covered, how to find student grades, or procedures for projects. You'll have all of this in one central location, so there's no need to share it on this night when you can speak with parents face to face.

You've got a (mostly) captive audience in front of you. They wouldn't be there if they didn't care about their child's education. They come to see who takes care of their child during the day. You need to speak about their *children*. In some cases, it's their only child. In many, it's their *baby*, no matter the age. Share what's important to you this year—that you want their children to become lifelong learners. You want to give their children time to practice *empathy*. Show them a video of their children, or last year's students. Then open it up for questions. Have a business card, bookmark, or follow up with an email with your class's website on it. If you can swing it, have your site open on school laptops or iPads where parents will be sitting. Have QR codes on tables that parents can scan to find your website and bookmark it—right on their phones. If a parent comes back for a conference during the year, sum up what you've already said about how your class runs in one or two sentences so your focus or goals for the year are clear once again.

> You'll find one of my Parent Night spiels on my blog:
> **tinyurl.com/ShiftParentNight.**

Continue the conversation—at least once a month.

At one of our Tech Academy days in my district, I went to an hour session put on by Jen Smith (@EdtechJenSmith), a tech guru in our district who helped me begin my own Genius Hour. She gave a few easy ways to keep parents updated—one of which I acted upon. I now use Animoto and a short blog post to share every two weeks with parents what we're doing in class: tinyurl.com/ShiftParentUpdates. (Better yet—still a shift I need to make—have your students write the blog post!) Students are the photographers, and their perspective on things helps parents see that not only are they learning, but they are happy. This is one item I spend my own money on. I purchase a $30 subscription each year to Animoto so I can make videos that are up to ten minutes long. (The free account allows for 30-second videos.) I'll happily pay $2.50 a month if it makes even three parents happy knowing more of what we're doing in class. They spread the word, and we know community news (good or bad) gets around fast. If parents are surprised when it comes time for conferences, it's not because you did not inform them. I was recently in a parent meeting where one parent thanked me for my updates and photos I put together every two weeks.

The other parent, however, said he never read them. I do what I can, and 50 percent of the parents being informed is much better than zero. I'd much rather be proactive than have to cover my behind after a parent gets upset about something. Been there, done that. Tough lesson learned!

I've learned from many mistakes. I have a feeling I'll forever be making mistakes. I hope I learn from each one, because the repercussions are so exhausting! A giant mistake was not communicating to parents early enough in the year. On my fortieth birthday, in a meeting with a parent and my principal, one parent said that what I was doing in my class was "crazy. And all the other parents think so too." It was like a punch in the gut. Thankfully, my principal had my back, and I was more determined than ever to do what I thought was right for the kids. My husband asked, "What are you going to do about it?" (Oh, how open-ended questions help us learn!) I resolved that "next year will be different," and it was, as I started letting parents know about our endeavors right from the first week. Our work became more transparent. Administration, parents, students, and anyone else on the Internet could see what we were doing and, better yet, the reasons why.

> See my quick reflection about dealing with upset
> parents here: **tinyurl.com/ShiftParentUpset.**

After the first quarter of each school year, I send out a quick survey (via Google Form) to parents. It's usually a simple request, such as, "Please let me know how you think our first quarter has gone." I clarify by saying, "Please include anything you've noticed: benefits, pitfalls, questions and/or concerns regarding your child and his/her class." I get anxious when I send the link to parents. The spreadsheet waits in the queue only minutes before I check it. Every few waking hours, I open it again for any new responses. Then this happens: I get eight (out of

66 possible) positive responses, one positive that includes a suggestion (hooray!), and one concerned (or even seemingly angry) parent. Where does my mind put all its brain power? My brain's gears whir around how I'm going to convince this parent that what we're doing is actually good and beautiful. I want this parent to get the "OMG, how has my child not been exposed to this in previous years" kind of thinking. It won't always happen. We *cannot* please everyone.

Hey—I *asked* for the feedback. Which responses teach me more? Which responses push me further? Which responses help me communicate better? You know the answer. We need some criticism to keep us grounded. We need some backlash to help us grow. I cannot be hypocritical. If I believe my students learn best from feedback, why wouldn't I learn best from feedback?! I will continue to ask parents (and students!) for their feedback—positive or not. Their responses will most likely deplete my energy. However, they will also help me grow, because I am a person who will act on this new information. I will improve in some fashion. My mom recently reminded me: "If you get no criticism, you have done nothing." Because criticism hurts, I just can't make myself go so far as to "welcome criticism." However, when you do receive it, both you and the parent will (hopefully) learn something new as you continue the conversation about what's best for their children.

COMMUNICATE WITH STUDENTS

Ah, yes. You may get some resistance from students! Those who are grade-driven and those who seem (to you) unmotivated may resist. Not one way of teaching is right for every child. There is no "cure-all." Keep talking the talk and walking the walk. Remember, you will be taking some students out of their comfort zone. Many are comfortable simply doing what they're told. They are used to complying with rules. They like the traditional methods. It works for them! They may not be used to teachers giving them choice, voice, and various responsibilities in the classroom. It could be stressful, making their year difficult. Help them have a voice by asking them to fill out a survey that is comparable to the one you send home to parents. After reading through their answers, have those one-on-one conversations with them regarding their concerns, or address the group as a whole if they have a question or suggestion that could benefit all of your students.

Throughout the year, keep encouraging students to try their best, share their questions and stories, and help one another learn as much as they can. Here are some phrases I say in class to continue the growth mindset in students:

» "It's not about the grade; it's about the learning."

» "Why not? Are you still being respectful to yourself and others? Then go for it."

» "How will this help us?" "How can you help?"

» "What will we learn by doing this?"

» "What's the point of this activity?" or "How could you learn from this activity?"

» "Why are we spending precious class time doing this?"

» "What do you think?" and "Why do you think this?"

» "What is a life lesson we've learned from this experience?"

Important to Note

You've only got 180 days or so to create a culture of learning each year with students. Getting to know your students isn't just about the walls, furniture, and activities. It's time spent really listening to them. When you ask them to answer a question, listen to their answers so that you can be responsive to their ideas. Do not let their answers and passions and ideas fall flat. Children of all ages are quick to learn if you are asking these questions for them—and for you. Shifts that give some choice and voice to students can either build relationships that will make your lessons stick better throughout the rest of the year, or you will risk losing student respect. It depends on if and how you respond to their inquiries and ideas. Respond to their ideas so they know they can trust you with their contributions.

COMMUNICATE WITH YOUR COWORKERS

I leave sharing with your coworkers for last, only because that's where I, personally, have felt the most resistance in the past. This seems to be the case with many teachers, in many school settings, and it makes me terribly sad. Why don't we feel we can share ideas in a safe environment, just as we are asking the students to do? Is it because some teachers think of it as a competition? Why would that be? Is it really all in my head because negative remarks sink in deeper than positive support? Perhaps. We are all so different, and when we encounter resistance regarding ideas we're trying, we need to remember that not every teaching style is best for every student. Our students need different teaching methods and philosophies.

That said, we should all want to improve by learning *with* and *from* one another. Teachers need to remember that their job is a career, and it should be a passion. We need to remember that we are lifelong learners, and that is the only way we'll keep doing what is right for students. Things are slowly changing in schools, but it's like turning around a battleship. It will take time. Heck, I'll most likely be retired by the time school is the way I really want it to be. It's also true that many teachers want change to happen, but they don't want to be the ones who need to change. Change, although desired by many, is difficult to implement for various reasons. We need to be cognizant of all perspectives.

I'm very fortunate to have the support of my administration. Only a few at my school know the shifts I've taken, and I feel like I'm on my own for many endeavors. Aren't we all? I blame myself—for not taking the time to share or ask for more help. I have found time to learn from and share with teachers online, but I haven't made much time to learn and share at my own school building. If I want more support, I need to share the reasons why I haven't waited around for things to change, and why I've made changes myself. This is tough to do during our busy days. Really—how much do you know of what's going on in a class down the hall? We need to make sharing in our own schools a priority. If we cannot make the time, we need to ask our administration for this time. I *have* taken the time to share with my co-teacher and my co-ELA teacher because I know doing so is a priority for *my* learning as much as it is for theirs.

If a coworker questions an idea you're sharing, express curiosity and listen to their concerns. Use the questions you've asked of yourself! You may be surprised at their concerns, and they may shine a light on issues you haven't considered yet. You may get closer to understanding their position when you ask a question such as, "What do you want to achieve?" Then ask them to tell you more. Take time to listen to coworkers, hear them out, then ask more questions. They will hopefully feel valued and will then take the time to listen to your ideas. One conversation I had with a teacher revolved around me not giving marks on every assignment. This teacher said, "Well, sure! I'd love to not give grades too! That would be so easy." I had not even thought that other teachers would think this terribly difficult shift I was putting myself through was easy! We didn't have time to discuss it then; I'm sure my mouth hung wide open as we walked our separate ways.

If you are still finding resistance, ask yourself, "What will happen if we stay the course?" If you don't like the answer, you need to try again. Explain why, even if the entire district isn't on board (yet), *you* need to change. Then ask for their support. What will work best for you is finding a partner in your school who will ask you guiding questions and play the devil's advocate. Then listen to him or her to find the cause of any fears of or resistance to change. Resistance to change is natural. If you are putting yourself out there, you are asking for people to question your ideas. Hopefully your coworkers will be curious enough to ask you important questions that will guide you to learning more about the subject or process. Their curiosity might even cause you to rethink something you're trying or prompt ideas to more efficiently accomplish your goals.

Share with your coworkers what you are doing that you believe is right for the students. Explain to them your struggles, and ask them what they're trying. Start the conversation, then keep it going. You may have to be the "keeper of the flame." There will be days you feel like you can't do any more, but you have to keep spreading the word if you believe the shifts you are making are right for children. Having your ideas questioned can feel exhausting and discouraging. I know. I've been there. But you need to keep sharing if you decide to not be one of those teachers who has her door closed all the time and never socializes with anyone anymore. I now ask questions that encourage thought and reflection. Then I listen to their responses and use those as a springboard.

Remember that you are in a different place than many teachers. You bring a different background and comfort level to conversations. It may take a long time, but we must slowly turn the ship (labeled "education") around. Complacency is dangerous. It is an inhibitor to growth. Question the status quo, and then offer suggestions! Our students were not born in the twentieth century. I believe we must change, along with our students, in order to perform our best. It's our responsibility.

FINAL THOUGHTS

If we're growing as educators, we'll find ourselves out of our comfort zone. This is another type of resistance. It's tough to try something new and fail or get knocked down a notch when you reflect. We're *learning* as we grow! If we're asking our students to challenge themselves as they learn, we should be challenging ourselves as well! There are physical growing pains, and I'm convinced there are mental growing pains. It's not easy. You will have resistance from others, and your own self may tell you it's just too difficult.

What's wonderfully positive is that you are not resistant to new ideas. You give them a try when things aren't going right. You're not being a frog. Let me explain. You can put a frog in a pot of water and put the pot on the stove. Frogs adapt to temperature change—so much so that if you slowly heat up the water to boiling, the frog will not try to escape. The frog will, instead, perish. By reading professional litera- ture, you are not sitting still. You are resistant to doing things the way you've always done them! You are exercising your brain, looking for new ideas for your students. This will get you far. You will *not* sit in the pot until you cook yourself. If (when) you encounter resistance, it will be with others who simply do not understand (yet) the reasons why you are making shifts in your classroom. The children are fortunate that you are open to new ideas, and that you will not just sit in the pot until you are cooked!

When I lead workshops or shorter presentations about personaliz- ing student learning, I encounter teachers who are worried about other teachers and administration not being supportive. I always include Elsa's lyrics to "Let It Go" from the movie *Frozen*. At one point, she sings, "I don't care what they're going to say. Let the storm rage on. The cold never bothered me anyway." What is this raging storm? Fear. We're scared. We're scared students will waste or even abuse this precious time given to them. We're scared we won't have time to fit these ideas into our curriculum. We're scared administration won't be supportive. We're scared other teachers will think we don't "teach" anymore.

More lyrics spout, "I don't care what they're going to say," yet we probably do. I care what people think of me. I know I shouldn't, and I'm comfortable in my skin, but I don't like cold shoulders—the cold *does* bother me. The risk takers in school are often ostracized. I'm now in the business of "faking it 'till I make it." I'm going to pretend that "the cold never bothered me anyway," since I'm doing this because I think *it's best for the kids.* It's not about me. And how should I get buy-in from other teachers if I feel I need it? Ask them for help. I let go of the idea that I need to do it all on my own.

When change is forced upon us, we cringe. We dig our heels in and don't follow easily. When it's **our** idea, however, and we get to control the circumstances, we run with it. We often jump in, whether we're ready or not! You have read this far. You want change. You need change in order to continue being happy with your career. Embrace the small shifts that help you attain that "dream class." It's not up to the kids. They're the reason you work as hard as you do. They're the reason you're still in the profession. You need to shift things around if you expect them to be engaged in your content and learn under your leadership. Other teachers will follow your lead. It's up to you to make the shifts and share with them your struggles and successes.

When I began writing out the ideas in this book, I started to realize I am ready to share the small shifts I've made in my own classroom because I trust in their value. Oh, sure, it's been a *long* journey to get the classroom culture I've come to cherish. I still have a long way to go, but each year has gone even better than the last! And yes, it's difficult when I have to start over with a new group of children each school year. I've learned to be patient and give them (and myself) time. Although it can be difficult, I see these shifts as critical to longevity in my career. I use them to balance out the negativity that we sometimes face in the media, and even in our own school district. I have many more years until retirement, and I need to make sure students are learning as much as they can each year. We can learn more when we have a culture of trust and respect. I cannot go back to the way I used to teach. It's not healthy for me or the children.

Hopefully other teachers will snatch up these ideas and share them, and soon they won't seem so "crazy." Soon they will be commonplace, and *children* will be leading in classrooms, learning more than ever. Teaching is the toughest thing I've ever done. Shifting my thinking and actions wasn't the easiest, either. However, teaching is also the most rewarding thing I've ever done—each time I see students learning from their own experiences or from one another, my heart flies out of my chest. Sometimes you need change in order to love your work again. Letting go of the control over every tiny detail has let my students grow right before my very eyes. When my students leave my care, my hope is that they will have a thirst for lifelong learning. THIS is what we should desire and work towards every single day. It is our duty as educators.

When my students leave my care, my hope is that they will have a thirst for lifelong learning.

FURTHER READING

Instead of asking you to read even more, I'd like to suggest you write. If you haven't yet, begin a blog of your own teaching journey. Reflect on what goes right and oh-so-terribly wrong, how you can improve for "next time," and questions you still have. (It's been a fun journey for me to read through the last four years of blog posts and see how far my thinking has come! You'll find more to read soon—online and in other books. I hope you then write to reflect on this learning as well.) If you're already a blogger, help spread the word of what you believe is best for kids, and keep the conversations going. Share your thinking about this book, and prompt the important conversations. Ask the thought-provoking questions! Let me know where you disagree with me or how you can make these ideas even stronger. We learn best by learning from one another. Let me know when you begin; I'm excited to learn from you!

REFLECTION AND CALL TO ACTION

» How will you cultivate your students' thirst for learning?

» How will you present your ideas to parents at the start of the year?

» How will you seek out feedback from students, their parents, and your peers?

» What plans do you have for sharing with parents throughout the rest of the year?

» What is your least favorite part of teaching—and why?

» How can you put the ownership on the students to take this on for you, at least in part?

» How will this make the culture in your classroom more geared towards learning?

» How will you decide to respond to resistance that will ultimately come your way?

_____

_____

_____

_____

_____

_____

MAKE THE FIRST SHIFT

Change doesn't have to be all or nothing. What will you try first? How will you share your failures and successes with others at your own school? How will you choose to share your failures and successes online?

How will you reflect on the shifts you're making in the classroom? Consider sharing on a platform where other educators can learn from your mistakes and successes.

Continue asking questions that drive your learning.

Let's keep the conversations going!

> ## Life is hard, but no matter what happens, we beat the drum and we dance again.
>
> —*Serafina's Promise* by Ann E. Burg

My dreams are coming true! Don't just imagine the class of your dreams. I hope you'll join me on this journey so we can have classroom cultures in which students become lifelong learners.

Acknowledgments

With gratitude to my family, who has always encouraged me to try whatever it is that floats my boat. When you look at me with that "You're bonkers!" look, I can take it, because I know you love me for who I am.

To my husband and soulmate who fills up my senses while helping all my dreams come true. I do not know where I'd be without you and your modeling. You have been there from the beginning of this classroom journey. You have read every blog post, helped (literally!) build our classroom library, created items for the kids to use and enjoy, supported me when I'm up and when I'm down, and asked me those critical questions that further my thinking. Thank you for taking care of me in the multitude of ways you find to do so. It's so fun when you ask, "What's next?"

To all those parents, educators, and administrators who have helped shape my beliefs and continue to challenge me to keep the shifts coming—all for the sake of learners in our charge.

And to all the students—past, present, and future—thank you for believing in me even though you know best that I don't have all the answers! You make me want to stay in school for many more years to come!

Bring the *Shift This!* Message to Your Organization or Event

Shift the Culture of Your Classroom

It all started when I gave students time to read—and then share what they were reading. Simple enough, right?! This was the catalyst that sparked the change in everything I did in the classroom. Four years later, you wouldn't recognize my classes. I don't decorate the room, student choice is ubiquitous, we have time built in to personalize learning, students teach one another, and we use feedback in lieu of grades. Join me as I share valuable **lessons learned** when I dedicated time during the week for students to learn what THEY wanted to learn.

What's the Hoopla Over Personalized Learning?

What's the big hoopla over Genius Hour and other forms of student-directed learning? Why hand over precious class time to the students? This session focuses on the many reasons WHY you should make time for student-directed learning in your classroom. If you are armed with the reasons why, you'll have no choice but to jump in yourself. Hold on tight for the journey ahead, as well as the shifts that will ultimately transform the rest of your teaching career!

Four-Hour Workshop Session

Why take time out of your curriculum for students to own the learning? You'll have time during this workshop to hammer out reasons WHY student-directed learning, such as Genius Hour, is vital. Time will also be used to explore comprehensive resources and create a plan for your classroom or school so students can pursue their passions. We'll figure out specific ways to tackle any obstacles together.

CONTACT FORM: SHIFTTHIS.WEEBLY.COM

More From

DBC INC. DAVE BURGESS Consulting, Inc.

Teach Like a PIRATE

Increase Student Engagement, Boost Your Creativity, and Transform Your Life as an Educator
By Dave Burgess (@BurgessDave)

Teach Like a PIRATE is the New York Times' best-selling book that has sparked a worldwide educational revolution. It is part inspirational manifesto that ignites passion for the profession, and part practical road map filled with dynamic strategies to dramatically increase student engagement. Translated into multiple languages, its message resonates with educators who want to design outrageously creative lessons and transform school into a life-changing experience for students.

Learn Like a PIRATE

Empower Your Students to Collaborate, Lead, and Succeed

By Paul Solarz (@PaulSolarz)

Today's job market demands that students be prepared to take responsibility for their lives and careers. We do them a disservice if we teach them how to earn passing grades without equipping them to take charge of their education. In *Learn Like a PIRATE*, Paul Solarz explains how to design classroom experiences that encourage students to take risks and explore their passions in a stimulating, motivating, and supportive environment where improvement, rather than grades, is the focus. Discover how student-led classrooms help students thrive and develop into self-directed, confident citizens who are capable of making smart, responsible decisions, all on their own.

P is for PIRATE

Inspirational ABC's for Educators

By Dave and Shelley Burgess (@Burgess_Shelley)

Teaching is an adventure that stretches the imagination and calls for creativity every day! In *P is for PIRATE*, husband and wife team Dave and Shelley Burgess encourage and inspire educators to make their classrooms fun and exciting places to learn. Tapping into years of personal experience and drawing on the insights of more than seventy educators, the authors offer a wealth of ideas for making learning and teaching more fulfilling than ever before.

Play Like a Pirate

Engage Students with Toys, Games, and Comics

by Quinn Rollins (@jedikermit)

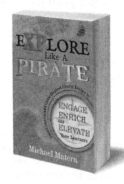

Yes! School can be simultaneously fun and educational. In *Play Like a Pirate*, Quinn Rollins offers practical, engaging strategies and resources that make it easy to integrate fun into your curriculum. Regardless of the grade level you teach, you'll find inspiration and ideas that will help you engage your students in unforgettable ways.

eXPlore Like a Pirate

Gamification and Game-Inspired Course Design to Engage, Enrich, and Elevate Your Learners

By Michael Matera (@MrMatera)

Are you ready to transform your classroom into an experiential world that flourishes on collaboration and creativity? Then set sail with classroom game designer and educator Michael Matera as he reveals the possibilities and power of game-based learning. In *eXPlore Like a Pirate*, Matera serves as your experienced guide to help you apply the most motivational techniques of gameplay to your classroom. You'll learn gamification strategies that will work with and enhance (rather than replace) your current curriculum and discover how these engaging methods can be applied to any grade level or subject.

Lead Like a PIRATE

Make School Amazing for Your Students and Staff

By Shelley Burgess and Beth Houf
(@Burgess_Shelley, @BethHouf)

In *Lead Like a PIRATE*, education leaders Shelley Burgess and Beth Houf map out the character traits necessary to captain a school or district. You'll learn where to find the treasure that's already in your classrooms and schools—and how to bring out the very best in your educators. This book will equip and encourage you to be relentless in your quest to make school amazing for your students, staff, parents, and communities.

The Zen Teacher

Creating FOCUS, SIMPLICITY, and TRANQUILITY in the Classroom

By Dan Tricarico (@TheZenTeacher)

Teachers have incredible power to influence—even improve—the future. In *The Zen Teacher*, educator, blogger, and speaker Dan Tricarico provides practical, easy-to-use techniques to help teachers be their best—unrushed and fully focused—so they can maximize their performance and improve their quality of life. In this introductory guide, Dan Tricarico explains what it means to develop a Zen practice—something that has nothing to do with religion and everything to do with your ability to thrive in the classroom.

Master the Media

How Teaching Media Literacy Can Save Our Plugged-in World

By Julie Smith (@julnilsmith)

Written to help teachers and parents educate the next generation, *Master the Media* explains the history, purpose, and messages behind the media. The point isn't to get kids to unplug; it's to help them make informed choices, understand the difference between truth and lies, and discern perception from reality. Critical thinking leads to smarter decisions—and it's why media literacy can save the world.

The Innovator's Mindset

Empower Learning, Unleash Talent,
and Lead a Culture of Creativity

By George Couros (@gcouros)

The traditional system of education requires students to hold their questions and compliantly stick to the scheduled curriculum. But our job as educators is to provide new and better opportunities for our students. It's time to recognize that compliance doesn't foster innovation, encourage critical thinking, or inspire creativity—and those are the skills our students need to succeed. In *The Innovator's Mindset*, George Couros encourages teachers and administrators to empower their learners to wonder, to explore—and to become forward-thinking leaders.

50 Things You Can Do with Google Classroom

By Alice Keeler and Libbi Miller
(@AliceKeeler, @MillerLibbi)

It can be challenging to add new technology to the classroom, but it's a must if students are going to be well-equipped for the future. Alice Keeler and Libbi Miller shorten the learning curve by providing a thorough overview of the Google Classroom App. Part of Google Apps for Education (GAfE), Google Classroom was specifically designed to help teachers save time by streamlining the process of going digital. Complete with screenshots, *50 Things You Can Do with Google Classroom* provides ideas and step-by-step instructions to help teachers implement this powerful tool.

50 Things to Go Further with Google Classroom

A Student-Centered Approach

By Alice Keeler and Libbi Miller
(@AliceKeeler, @MillerLibbi)

Today's technology empowers educators to move away from the traditional classroom where teachers lead and students work independently—each doing the same thing. In *50 Things to Go Further with Google Classroom: A Student-Centered Approach*, authors and educators Alice Keeler and Libbi Miller offer inspiration and resources to help you create a digitally rich, engaging, student-centered environment. They show you how to tap into the power of individualized learning that is possible with Google Classroom.

Pure Genius

*Building a Culture of Innovation and
Taking 20% Time to the Next Level*

By Don Wettrick (@DonWettrick)

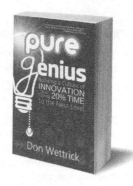

For far too long, schools have been bastions of boredom, killers of creativity, and way too comfortable with compliance and conformity. In *Pure Genius*, Don Wettrick explains how collaboration—with experts, students, and other educators—can help you create interesting, and even life-changing, opportunities for learning. Wettrick's book inspires and equips educators with a systematic blueprint for teaching innovation in any school.

140 Twitter Tips for Educators

*Get Connected, Grow Your Professional
Learning Network, and Reinvigorate Your Career*

By Brad Currie, Billy Krakower, and Scott Rocco
(@bradmcurrie, @wkrakower, @ScottRRocco)

Whatever questions you have about education or about how you can be even better at your job, you'll find ideas, resources, and a vibrant network of professionals ready to help you on Twitter. In *140 Twitter Tips for Educators* #Satchat hosts and founders of Evolving Educators, Brad Currie, Billy Krakower, and Scott Rocco offer step-by-step instructions to help you master the basics of Twitter, build an online following, and become a Twitter rock star.

Ditch That Textbook

*Free Your Teaching and Revolutionize
Your Classroom*

By Matt Miller (@jmattmiller)

Textbooks are symbols of centuries-old education. They're often outdated as soon as they hit students' desks. Acting "by the textbook" implies compliance and a lack of creativity. It's time to ditch those textbooks—and those textbook assumptions about learning! In *Ditch That Textbook*, teacher and blogger Matt Miller encourages educators to throw out meaningless, pedestrian teaching and learning practices. He empowers them to evolve and improve on old, standard teaching methods. *Ditch That Textbook* is a support system, toolbox, and manifesto to help educators free their teaching and revolutionize their classrooms.

How Much Water Do We Have?

5 Success Principles for Conquering Any Change and Thriving in Times of Change

by Pete Nunweiler with Kris Nunweiler

In *How Much Water Do We Have?* Pete Nunweiler identifies five key elements—information, planning, motivation, support, and leadership—that are necessary for the success of any goal, life transition, or challenge. Referring to these elements as the 5 Waters of Success, Pete explains that, like the water we drink, you need them to thrive in today's rapidly paced world. If you're feeling stressed out, overwhelmed, or uncertain at work or at home, pause and look for the signs of dehydration. Learn how to find, acquire, and use the 5 Waters of Success—so you can share them with your team and family members.

Instant Relevance

Using Today's Experiences in Tomorrow's Lessons

By Denis Sheeran (@MathDenisNJ)

Every day, students in schools around the world ask the question, "When am I ever going to use this in real life?" In *Instant Relevance*, author and keynote speaker Denis Sheeran equips you to create engaging lessons *from* experiences and events that matter to your students. Learn how to help your students see meaningful connections between the real world and what they learn in the classroom—because that's when learning sticks.

The Classroom Chef

Sharpen Your Lessons. Season Your Classes. Make Math Meaningful.

By John Stevens and Matt Vaudrey (@Jstevens009, @MrVaudrey)

In *The Classroom Chef*, math teachers and instructional coaches John Stevens and Matt Vaudrey share their secret recipes, ingredients, and tips for serving up lessons that engage students and help them "get" math. You can use these ideas and methods as-is, or better yet, tweak them and create your own enticing educational meals. The message the authors share is that, with imagination and preparation, every teacher can be a Classroom Chef.

Start. Right. Now.

Teach and Lead for Excellence

By Todd Whitaker, Jeff Zoul, and Jimmy Casas
(@ToddWhitaker, @Jeff_Zoul, @casas_jimmy)

In their work leading up to *Start. Right. Now.* Todd Whitaker, Jeff Zoul, and Jimmy Casas studied educators from across the nation and discovered four key behaviors of excellence: Excellent leaders and teachers *Know the Way, Show the Way, Go the Way, and Grow Each Day.* If you are ready to take the first step toward excellence, this motivating book will put you on the right path.

The Writing on the Classroom Wall

How Posting Your Most Passionate Beliefs about Education Can Empower Your Students, Propel Your Growth, and Lead to a Lifetime of Learning

By Steve Wyborney (@SteveWyborney)

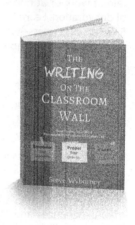

In *The Writing on the Classroom Wall*, Steve Wyborney explains how posting and discussing Big Ideas can lead to deeper learning. You'll learn why sharing your ideas will sharpen and refine them. You'll also be encouraged to know that the Big Ideas you share don't have to be profound to make a profound impact on learning. In fact, Steve explains, it's okay if some of your ideas fall *off* the wall. What matters most is sharing them.

LAUNCH

Using Design Thinking to Boost Creativity and Bring Out the Maker in Every Student

By John Spencer and A.J. Juliani
(@spencerideas, @ajjuliani)

Something happens in students when they define themselves as *makers* and *inventors* and *creators*. They discover powerful skills—problem-solving, critical thinking, and imagination—that will help them shape the world's future … our future. In *LAUNCH*, John Spencer and A.J. Juliani provide a process that can be incorporated into every class at every grade level … even if you don't consider yourself a "creative teacher." And if you dare to innovate and view creativity as an essential skill, you will empower your students to change the world—starting right now.

Kids Deserve It!

*Pushing Boundaries and Challenging
Conventional Thinking*

By Todd Nesloney and Adam Welcome
(@TechNinjaTodd, @awelcome)

In *Kids Deserve It!*, Todd and Adam encourage you to think big and make learning fun and meaningful for students. Their high-tech, high-touch, and highly engaging practices will inspire you to take risks, shake up the status quo, and be a champion for your students. While you're at it, you just might rediscover why you became an educator in the first place.

Escaping the School Leader's Dunk Tank

How to Prevail When Others Want to See You Drown

By Rebecca Coda and Rick Jetter
(@RebeccaCoda, @RickJetter)

No school leader is immune to the effects of discrimination, bad politics, revenge, or ego-driven coworkers. These kinds of dunk-tank situations can make an educator's life miserable. By sharing real-life stories and insightful research, the authors (who are dunk-tank survivors themselves) equip school leaders with the practical knowledge and emotional tools necessary to survive and, better yet, avoid getting "dunked."

Your School Rocks...So Tell People!

*Passionately Pitch and Promote the
Positives Happening on Your Campus*

By Ryan McLane and Eric Lowe
(@McLane_Ryan, @EricLowe21)

Great things are happening in your school every day. The problem is, no one beyond your school walls knows about them. School principals Ryan McLane and Eric Lowe want to help you get the word out! In *Your School Rocks ... So Tell People!* McLane and Lowe offer more than seventy immediately actionable tips along with easy-to-follow instructions and links to video tutorials. This practical guide will equip you to create an effective and manageable communication strategy using social media tools. Learn how to keep your students' families and community connected, informed, and excited about what's going on in your school.

Teaching Math with Google Apps

50 G Suite Activities

By Alice Keeler and Diana Herrington
(@AliceKeeler, @mathdiana)

Google Apps give teachers the opportunity to interact with students in a more meaningful way than ever before, while G Suite empowers students to be creative, critical thinkers who collaborate as they explore and learn. In *Teaching Math with Google Apps*, educators Alice Keeler and Diana Herrington demonstrate fifty different ways to bring math classes into to the twenty-first century with easy-to-use technology.

Table Talk Math

A Practical Guide for Bringing Math into Everyday Conversations

By John Stevens (@Jstevens009)

Making math part of families' everyday conversations is a powerful way to help children and teens learn to love math. In *Table Talk Math*, John Stevens offers parents (and teachers!) ideas for initiating authentic, math-based conversations that will get kids notice and be curious about all the numbers, patterns, and equations in the world around them.

About the Author

Joy Kirr is sought after for her workshops on how to bring student-directed learning into the classroom. Currently teaching seventh graders in a truly supportive district in Arlington Heights, Illinois, Joy is passionate about students owning their learning. She enjoys being known as a "Genius Hour Evangelist," and is grateful for how her students have stepped up their learning while giving and receiving feedback in lieu of grades. Presenting around the nation has helped Joy spread the message that educators need to strive for all children to become lifelong learners.

Joy earned her bachelor's degree in special education with an emphasis on deaf and hard-of-hearing in 1995, and she later earned her master's degree in reading from Northern Illinois University. Recently, she was nominated for a Golden Apple award for excellence and teaching in Illinois. Joy has been a National Board Certified Teacher since 2007.

CPSIA information can be obtained
at www.ICGtesting.com
Printed in the USA
BVOW06s1911280917
496224BV00010B/294/P